Conten

GW00361666

VOL 93   NO 1   SPRING

Poems

Richard Price		4, 9
Ken Smith		5
Annemarie Austin		7
John Latta		8
Lavinia Greenlaw		12
Beverley Bie Brahic		15
Michael Murphy		18
Simon Smith		20
Jonathan Treitel		24
Rachel Wetzsteon		26
David Wheatley		27
Jeremy Reed		28
Ed Barrett		29
Robert Stein		42

Essays

Richard Price	Generosity	44
David Ellis	D. H. Lawrence	50

Reviews

Robert Potts	Keston Sutherland, *Antifreeze*, *The Rictus Flag*, *Quid* magazine	58
Sarah Maguire	Saadi Simawe, *Modern Poetry in Translation No.19: Iraqi Poetry Today*	64
Andrea Brady	R. F. Langley, *More or Less*	67
Peter Manson	David Kinloch, *Un Tour D'Ecosse*	73
William Corbett	Tom Raworth, *Collected Poems*	75
Jan Montefiore	Stephen Burt, *Randall Jarrell and his Age*	78
Deryn Rees-Jones	Glyn Maxwell, *The Nerve*	79
Jane Griffiths	John McAuliffe, *A Better Life*	81
	Dennis O'Driscoll, *Exemplary Damages*	
	Medbh McGuckian, *The Face of the Earth*	

Stewart Brown   E. A. Markham, *A Rough Climate*   85
Andrew Duncan   Edwin Morgan, *Cathures: New Poems 1997–2001*   87
Simon Jenner   David Kennedy, *The President of Earth*   89
                       Michael Hulse, *Empires and Holy Lands:*
                       Poems 1976–2000
                       John Matthias, *Working Progress, Working Title*
James Keery   David Jones, *Wedding Poems*   91
Stephen Burt   Daniel Huws, *The Quarry*   93
Tony Curtis   R. S. Thomas, *Residues*   95
                       Roland Mathias, *Collected Poems*
                       Sheenagh Pugh, *The Beautiful Lie*
                       Sarah Corbett, *The Witch Bag*
                       Paul Henry, *The Slipped Leash*
                       John Davies, *North by South: New and Selected Poems*
                       Elin ap Hywel and Graham Davies, *Ffiniau/Borders*
John Redmond   Sophie Hannah, *First of the Last Chances*   100
                       John Whitworth, *The Whitworth Gun*
                       Anne Stevenson, *A Report from the Border*
                       Julian Turner, *Crossing the Outskirts*
                       Kevin Hart, *Flame Tree: Selected Poems*

Poet in the Gallery

Karlien van den Beukel   *Exodus: Photographs by Sebastião Salgado*   104

Art

Roy Arenella   46, 54
Ben E. Watkins   63, 77
Sebastião Salgado   106, 107

National Poetry Competition   108
Editorial Notelet   112
Contributors' Notes   113

Poems

Richard Price

A NEWS

I'm low, and the news . . .
has purchase.

That's nothing.

I've said nothing
for years: the life

of a child, hear-tell
a plague.

You are
so generous

with your silence.

You.

(I have news. Is it
news?

Good news?)

Ken Smith

SEAFARER

landward mountains and mountains, upended strata
tipped all the way up the coastline of what was
an almost country, almost Yugoslavia. Islands
that are mountains in the sea, the same in the same
dark blue waters the ancient wanderer spread sail on,
ten years lost, the waves cresting the same, bright
sunlight's swift jewellery forming and fast fading,
wind never willing enough, always far from home.
Not even almost there, the boat's wake always behind him.
So if not home then some haven beyond the next headland,
round the next cape almost, sunlight striding the sea
receding always into sea haze and more distance.

Home to his ancient dog and the wife's endless weaving,
not to mention the slaughterhouse he soon made of it.
Tales told round fires, late night yarns over alcohol,
trying some sense to this endless confusion of water.
Waves, tentative, foam crests soon falling, seamen
staring the sea down for some place looks like home
and the stars above in the right configurations,
wind whipped and sea blind, he sees in the sea's skin
forever on the move sight of the sun through pines
in the bright sea's reflections as it once was on land,
the motion the same as the same wind's back home,
almost. The endless immensity of longing for home.

Almost. Rocks, trees, beasts, faces of the familiar,
rearing from stone, out of water, wood, smoke, rock, clouds,
out of yesterday's brisk trade in the town, flash ahead of him,
gone. And below where light strikes, snakes, almost,
creatures writhing away into seaspray and light shine.
Words on the sea. Light's brief brilliant reflections,
languages never learned, cuneiform, glagolitic, Hebrew,
Arabic, glyphs, runes, living almost into letters, tongues,
alphabets, lost in the quick calligraphy of wind and water.
The almost everything almost always is, or boils down to:
it was or it will be, could be, may be, might be, perhaps,
though doubtful. Uncertain. World on the brink of itself.

Always almost always making it, becoming itself,
being or not being, uncertain of itself. Potential, say.
Out on the sea for instance where our seafarer
almost always is. Off the bitter coast. Off Hvar
and Korcula, birthplace it says here im Deutsch
of Antenor of Troy, and of Marco the Polo, wanderer
by land to the earth's ends and limits. Or by Ogygia,
Mijet now, a long lumpy island wherein seven
of ten lost years went by: cloudy light, forest,
a single road looping the gaps, *Ah Ithaca, where
are my olives, my olive trees?* Ogygia: upright rocks,
stoney warriors armed to the teeth, no landing there.

All this, blind, long after, Homer saw.

Annemarie Austin

AVOIDED SUBJECT

What I am avoiding will not be in this poem.
But you know the war museum is right below
the clouds Cornelia Parker photographed
with the camera of Hoess of Auschwitz –
whom we suppose more likely to have snapped
fields of buttercups than gas chambers.
I pressed the vetches picked from between
preserved huts at Birkenau, but also entered
each long darkness pungent with the chemicals
that kept woodrot at bay. They were needed –
the ground was boggy in August – but that phrase
is compromised in the context, it's as if
I'm meaning something else. Menace is a given,
though the fear of crime's far worse, they say,
(for now and for us) than statistics justify.
The house next door stood unoccupied for months
and no one broke in to rummage through
the displayed possessions – clothes and cooking pots
and spectacles and satchels not in glass cases.
Combing my hair at the window, I watch for
thunderheads to rise above the seaward roofs
loaded with hail that falls out of the chimney
onto my hearth as fat spots of liquid soot.

John Latta

TWO POEMS

1

Broken stalk of pepperweed, pointed arch
In blue snow. Winter is hanging on by its mean teeth.
Pine hills used to be here.

Depiction is our foolish game.
One lone deer entered the city by its southernmost gate, stood
Stock still, fetched up the usual comments and commands.

In another version a sentimental lassitude drowned out
Our own snowy blank federations of words, made us
Eat hearty, push back our chairs, and set to

Some serious smoking.

2

The long side of nothing is a hypotenuse, a shim
Jammed under the leading demarcations (linear)
Where being meets knowing and occasions a right industry.

Picture that. My one and only constituency
Language, its unflappability, its wondrous blunder.
Wisdom resides in the plunder

Play holds like a hand of poker in its fatty pink fist.
You think I'm bluffing. I am bluffing. Call me. You'll find me
Pulchritude itself, and mild, my metaphysical head lodging

Like a cavity in my musical mouth.

Richard Price

SOFTENED, BRIGHT

Computer light improves any painting,
back-lit for a radiant show.
Vermeer's balance, even, and jewellery
glistenise, but remain
in their glisten.

The casual folds – those drapes –
stay in their crease, a near crease,
but they know fabric now
as memories can think they know
what was best, what was
likely true.

Back-lit in a virtual exhibition:
I haven't a single picture of you
(days that did know what a day was),
can't now.

Softened, bright. It's so good
to have the, to have the technology.

FOLD-UP

Goodbye now Frank O'Hara, you were sweet

Donny, remember that remainder shop in Soho –
you'd just bought me *Damned to Fame*
The Life of Samuel Beckett
and I said not two weeks previous
I'd been propositioned
by a woman a few minutes off duty,
for a laugh I guess,
right in front of the Taschen Klimt?

Ian Brown, ex Stone Roses,
rides a fold-up bicycle backwards,
I think right by it, in a video
for a single called "Fear".
It's an acrostic song –
For Everyone A Road, and so on,
not bad going for pop culture,
though it's not always
one word per line (reminds me
of Roy Fisher's abc
in one of Ron King's exquisite pop-ups,
and how "Auld Lang Syne"
was once the tune all America
learned the alphabet to,
not that that's a nationalist statement,
and then there's Ellen, counting –
how sixes and sevens
are elided if she's not thinking –
it's the sibilant –
"She is only two years old!" –
so she'll go four, five, six, eight,
almost the kind of counting
Tom Robinson sang about
just before coming out,

a long time before
presenter material,
and Katie's teacher is saying
she thinks yes maybe Katie
can recognise one to three
(it's eye-pointing, mainly),
and we'll have to watch
the imbalance
between sides of the rib-cage,
first signs of scoliosis already there,
quite possibly, "classic symptoms",
but Jackie's already
got the facts, met other parents).

When Ian Brown pedals
backwards for miles –
it must be Berwick Street
and environs – all the pedestrians
are in reverse, too,
blurred –

if I can get our recorder to work
I'll tape it and see how it looks
as you rewind it. Of course,
you'll not get the music –
you'll just have to remember how it goes.
Not your kind of tune anyway.
Meet you there on Wednesday morning? Say Eleven?

Lavinia Greenlaw

A DAMSEL IN DISTRESS

after Wodehouse

whom she met without	had exhibited at times
she thoroughly disapproved	she had always felt sure
He, at least, she always felt	to injure the family

is the only one that offers	assuming – that is
beast desire	

by no other spot except	Here your lover may wander
to nobody, by nobody	at the end

righteous indignation	might be judicious to continue
he held the opinion that	so became him as this assault
who in his time had	of youth, had come to lock
as scarcely human	you've never got

a common rowdy in the streets	name in the papers
'If you knew the circumsta'	'The circumstances? They
are in print'	

THE SUN SESSIONS

after Otis Blackwell

'56.
Amphibious,
barely out of his tail.

Heart in his mouth. Don't.
Perhaps he is trying
to swallow it.

The bull-frogs on backing
inflate. Be true. Oo oo oo.
On the tough acoustic

of an empty pool. Don't.
To a heart. Doo wah.
That's cruel. Sha la la la.

De dum. I mean
cruel. Wo wo wo wo.
And true.

HUSH…

Where the fire of the making of a world
burns itself out, ash banks and rises.

Trees lay down their green.
Roofs lay down their houses.

A boy with a reed for a backbone
shakes in his bed.

It is to him that the mountain has spoken.
He must write in ash what the mountain said.

Beverley Bie Brahic

STROKE, APHASIA

With tremulous heads, the little red hens
sprint for the fence.
Cu-uut cut cut? they inquire. *Cuu-ut cut cut*, I reply,
and bang the door of the car. Now
they'll rephrase their question.

This a language I think I could learn:
singsong for anxious chickens,
vocables to calm the dog. A lexicon
of emphasis and drawn-out silences.
Perhaps I am glad you can no longer speak.

We tap the spoon against your chin.
Your mouth opens.
We void the spoon into that space.
Mouth we say. *More cake?* Or, *good dog?*
After a while it goes down.

The question is always the same question.
It's not the answer, it's the tone of voice.
Words only make suffering
more precise. For hunger any lover will tell you
gutturals are quite as effective.

They say you understand everything still,
but I don't know. Red hens quizz me
as yearningly, and what does a hen know?
We hold our breath and watch you sleep,
watch your body fill its lungs.

Your jaw drops, your arms relinquish
what they were cradling. Air enters your nose
and mouth suckingly
like the flux and reflux of an ocean –
like life itself and you its object.

Like the clatter of reeds, thinking the thoughts
they have no words for. The reeds
watch us go by and nod. *Hello. Good-bye.*
Come again. It is all we need to hear.
It is enough reality.

There's a hole in your charcoal grey mittens
darned with white thread: a snowflake has drifted
to your knuckle and will not melt.
Your hands are icy – they are, I felt them.
As cold as pebbles, as gravel, as claws.

THE SLEEP OF THE MAGI

The Magi are sleeping their stone sleep
on a pillar in Autun Cathedral.
They have kept their crowns on.
Their eyes are closed like oblivious smiles.

Except for this one, the one on top,
whose bare arm is out of the rippled coverlet
(someone tossed a pebble and the ripples spread
till they bounced off the edges
fraying a little, like a bedtime story):
warm shoulder, plump forearm, dimpled knuckles, fingers
        joined, thumb separate –
and wide eyes staring into the dark.

It's the look you would have if you woke in a strange place
and tried to remember where you were
and how you got there
and what it was that woke you.
It's the look you would have
if someone turned the light on suddenly,
and poked you in the shoulder
and pointed to the Star, which looks like a daisy.

I guess it must have gone behind a cloud
and they lay down to wait for it to clear up, so knackered
        after all their walking
the Angel had to come and wake them.

Michael Murphy

SPLINTERS

St Lucy's Day. Dark-room of the year. Moon burns on a slower fuse,
Earth's a pilgrim shadow crossing her face.

*

This season I'm wearing, buttoned up against the cold,
a dead man's hand-me-downs, someone else's metaphors:

*

Inside our pelts we live, brooding on love and spring –
the soul's green ice becoming grass, a sunlit park, hazy evenings.

*

Frost snaps. Trousers, shirt and socks hung out to dry
kick up a stiff-limbed can-can on the backyard washing line.

*

April. Every year it gets harder, remembering to forget
her face, woozy with diazepam, as she waits on the hospital steps.

*

Hand-written in my copy of Perec's *Un homme qui dort*, her words
have slept, stockpiling dust, breathing must: "Slumberously yours."

*

Touching harmonics from a glass, I think of her
mixing a large gin, mindful not to bruise the juniper.

*

Each day its little deaths: a hundred hairs, innumerable cells,
all the love we hid from others and ourselves,

*

the emptied sleeves of a cotton dress, weightless
on the back of a chair . . . What was said remains. The rest is silence.

*

Three floors up, curtains sashaying in the breeze of a fan,
two lovers are coming to the end of love. That's life. Walk on.

*

Whistling in the dark, balanced on the knife edge
of a railway track, a man walks backwards, the world going off in his
head.

*

The sharper we focus on love, the harsher light's vernacular,
the more we see each snapshot as a way of forgetting to remember

*

like a word the moment it's said: a wet handprint on baked stone
bleeding dry in the penitential blaze of afternoon.

Simon Smith

SLIPS LIGHT

A white "YOU" printed across my red tee-shirt in arial
Parked car then what
Do you think rushes here fits
There the message stops
How it then adds Michelle

DAY ONE

Walked straight
Into sound
Reflecting wave how to use it pull
Anything from your pocket anything
I'll guess right and it'll stick there
Michelle too
Into a sentence sign after
Sign after sign the cloud is
Like a white wing is like a white
Cloud and will it won't parked
Car same day same cloud
As Michelle says

PUTS YOU IN THE PICTURE

The index behind always leads to white knuckles and poor reflection
If you need more evidence come out with what you see
A white "YOU" printed across my red tee-shirt in arial
Flipped completely when Michelle goes you go early evening sun mid-September

WHO'S WHOSE

Echo. Sense of it carries back as a "hello".
More polish. What we want. More spit.
For which there is no evidence. Me peering back
Steer by other stars. What's that buzzing noise?
Stop it. It's irritating. Spicer's listening in. For which
There is none. Not a mirror. Not a moon.
Not an understanding. Funny little thing.
Everyone knows everyone in this explanation.
Goodbye with your heel. Echo the go.

REALITY

Doesn't always end up in the same place
Not always where were we
Sparkling where we were language is
Not optional as you pop it in you mouth
People wear stupid shoes in reality. Or Lego.
Rules finish with my heart and give me backache
A doorway sped toward
Ahem Michelle constructed out of surveillance and vertigo
I mean video
Walk towards me and I'm not there
Consistent with water damage
Worked out on ruled paper and too much
To carry Michelle signifies "made up"
Reality is a note

WARM RAIN

Let's play with things I think about when you went keep going
Infinity is roly-poly with Death at the end of it not a detail
Missed hot wet new dark
Marks where a chair scraped the grey snow-bright wall
Then off a cliff is knowing where to stop "thank you" in chorus is
To throw it away leave it to me sit tight as square is to sway more
Unstable not less
People don't think in sentences people think in puffa jackets
My glaze is a notebook my gaze is an email sick of now not
Taking "things" in
Who's in who's out who's paying
Drops over off out up and that's what

LOCAL COLOUR

Open out to white dead air
Work in neutral I'm doing stuff
Round the house I know
It's hardly there it is let it
Run the next day wakes up
And floats about fresh air
Air freshener smells like
It is stopped up in language
And is real
At last the Real doesn't last
Only in quotes or the houses of the rich
Face the echo bright and drop
To touch my toes not any
Kind of thing
My kind of thing you know

WEIGHT PROBLEM

Thick pencil, 4B or 6B close
 So I know where you are
To the graphite line black
Endings no not black echo
Or ripple like black back that's it
Left hand swings right foot drags
Past the corner then gone
Work out from notebook to step
Left with a cough
Dropped between I'm going
To enjoy this "sss" pulled
Sharp between front
Teeth see? And you do don't you
Need to drive far to find out
Watch closely shining grey

Jonathan Treitel

MY OWN HANDS

You are speaking to the man who lost his mittens in Sweden.
I hope whosoever found my mittens in Sweden
has exceptionally warm fingers even as we speak.
I know it is colder in Sweden than it is in many other places
where I myself might happen to be. It is not as if
I had forgotten my right hand on a bench in the waiting room
at the railway station in Gothenburg, and my left hand also.

INCARNATIONS

Somebody said I said, "When I was a mosquito . . . " Actually I said
"student". How anyone can mishear "student" as "mosquito"
is beyond me. (I know I mumble, but even so.)
Me, I would never take a student for a mosquito although
both have a hiss in the beginning and near the end the tongue flaps
                                        just behind the teeth.
Besides there is little to say about my life as a mosquito:
I buzzed, sucked, earned my Ph.D. in an arcane specialization
of which I retain little, and less
with every passing lifetime.

POEM TO BE PRINTED ON A T-SHIRT

A certain poet had eyes for my T-shirt.
'That's a nice T-shirt you have on,' she said
oh so casually. 'It is, isn't it?'
I replied. 'Matter of fact, I bought it
in a thrift store in a faraway city . . . '

Conversation drifted inconclusively.
I liked her. She liked my T-shirt.
A basis, maybe, for a relationship?

What happened thereafter, whether or not
we – well, anything . . . is more than I care
to put in verse.
                        Readers desirous
of further details, please send
a stamped, self-addressed postcard with
'T-SHIRT' only
in block capitals on the back.

Wait thirty days for delivery.
When it fails to arrive, your mourning is over.

Rachel Wetzsteon

from THIRTY-THREE

In or out of the loop, I *was* the loop,
a shiny trainset zooming around the room.

But like wind that loses itself in an alley and
is found, days later, turning upon itself,

like the woman who cries on her couch for an hour
then looks in a mirror and cries some more,

so moved is she by her own smeared features,
like the dream in which I was both judge

and applicant for a major prize,
self-reliance has an underside,

a silence that real storms, fierce tears,
strange dreams, with their rash explosions

rightly deride: oh break the stiff ring,
surprises I never saw coming, dismantle

and save me, lover the loop excluded,
sitting an acre, a table, a touch away.

David Wheatley

MACAW

Because the terrible hook-nosed scarlet macaw
will not leave me in peace I bring him tributes
of sliced fruit he scatters in raucous disdain,
whistle him tunes he knows far better than me,
begin sentences he interrupts me
to finish. Because he will as soon
have my eyes out as look at me through
the swivelling molluscs of his own two eyes
I cower and will myself small as the ripple
I make in his darting, aqueous humour
but in he dives after me into the black
pool of his stare and will not rest until
his maggot tongue has slimed the hand
he perches atop and he has trodden hand,
shoulder and head beneath his standstill march
and opened his wings over my head
to stand for a moment, the terrible wingspan
doing its clipped, furious worst as I cower
and cover my eyes in the black shadow
of every last scarlet, blue and green feather
and 'help!' try to shout, dummy to his ventriloquist,
'help!', and screeching he interrupts me
for the whole street to hear, 'Help help help!'

Jeremy Reed

EXILE IN LA

The ambiguous Mancunian
points up his silver Porsche into a sun
cored orange over Mexico.

He listens to his own demos,
morose inflections winningly
smalltowning it to Sunset Boulevard.

Back home his aesthetic's austerity.
A giant silver cross altars a theme
to which the quiffy occupant aspires,

his solo life reviewed by Steve McQueen
bare-torsoed in a nippled photograph.
The singer's disaffected from his roots –

a busless Salford on grainy Sundays,
his Englishness romancing pop,
glitzing a sparkle to life's small complaints . . .

His exile's fed by attitude,
the dispossessed kinging a leather chair
in Scott Fitzgerald's breakdown sanctuary,

the soft-mouthed writer louchely cocktailing
each drink towards him like a loaded gun.
Mozza's Gatsby's "This Charming Man" –

hookily, declarative, period song.
LA frissons inside his chemistry;
the silence in his courtyard's tangible,

as though a slab of time came there to rest
before returning to the pressure-zone.
His vintage jeans are 1950's-bashed,

paired with a velvet Gucci tuxedo.
His solitude's blued by the ocean's blues,
he waits appropriately on the world's edge.

Ed Barrett

BARBARA STANWYCK HAD WARDROBE SHOW HER STOMACH

for Beverly Corbett

Barbara Stanwyck had wardrobe show her stomach but asked them to cover up the
rest of her body, which she said was flawed. Can you hear her saying "flawed" in a
Brooklyn accent? Description wants to cup your face in its hands, cradle a
telephone in the crook of its transparent arm, whispering, "It's impossible to
know," and "We all stand revealed." Barbara Stanwyck had wardrobe describe her
body according to her body's logic: "Give a girl a break, will ya? Yeah, like that.
Aw, you're a peach!" And description wants to know the impossible too, set it
down for the record, a silver ribbon studded with rhinestones. If you're lucky, you
hear someone mean it in terms of a clarity of feeling: "I'd do anything for you" –
not totally "out there" or anything too deported from the laity of believers and the
truths they take by the hand where a diamond cutout over the midriff shows
Barbara Stanwyck's stomach. "Why now?", it goes in the dark, "Why, when
everything was just beginning to change, my life on track again?" To cradle her
body with clarity and deportment is all she was asking in her crooked accent,
embracing wardrobe like a doll, a living doll.

ANNIVERSARY YEARS

for Michael and Isabel Pinto-Franco

These are the kind of years we don't mind adding on because they also add up in a sweet way, like pitchforks full of hay until you have a haystack big enough to feed a herd of cows or set on fire as a signal in the night sky – the haystack, not the cows: setting cows on fire is unkind and illegal and an image I will not let into this poem, not even as a signal in the night sky for sailors in danger off the coast. Goodbye, cows on fire – and don't bump into anything flammable on your way out the door as you amble to the Charles River where you can douse those flames which are only imaginary, so you're not really getting burned: I wouldn't do that to you although hot milk for cocoa is yummy, so if you could squeeze off a quart before you go . . . No, you'd better leave, lighting the way as you shamble into Porter Square, carrying milk and flames through the snow falling on all those stupid shoppers at Star Market who don't realize how many sailors' lives are hanging on your every move.

FLIGHT INTO EGYPT

I saw former Red Sox pitcher Bill "The Spaceman" Lee take something from a dumpster in front of the Corbett house. "Watch it!" said Lee, "dreams are not hard science like colonoscopy and laser hair removal – dreams don't even know your name, Mr. Wally Cox, and therefore they come to you but could just as easily visit someone else when all you wanted was to have your head patted like a child. And I am Bill Lee, making a voodoo doll of Carl Yazstremski whose dream came to me by mistake and said Yaz was living in the Corbett house, upstairs under the eaves." "Is Bill moving?" I asked, "What's he need a dumpster for, anyway?" "Ask him yourself, here he comes," shouted Bill Lee as he ran down Columbus Avenue, sideways like a crab. "Bill, I don't understand, what is this all about?" "Dreams," snarled Corbett, "Who the hell is Bill Lee to talk about dreams!" And we walked into his study which was filled with life-size voodoo dolls of Bill Lee, each wearing a different set of legs: deer legs, grasshopper legs, rat's feet, and still twitching in the corner, a doll with legs of a blue claw crab taken from the Gowanus Canal when Bill was visiting Brooklyn where the crab population, long crushed under the weight of pollution, now floats and copulates in the currents around Brooklyn like a blue halo. "Dreams know your name, Ed Cullen Bryant, like a real estate agent knows a price. Through my black art I torment Bill Lee with more sets of legs climbing up on him than some of the poor souls who once worked as prostitutes on Columbus Avenue – But now Boston has these dumpsters where our true past, which is unclaimed dreams, gets shoveled out each morning!" And Bill kicked the side of the dumpster so hard some trash spilled out revealing a child's Burger King paper crown from a lost day in the lost life of the nameless real, its gold paper glistening in the sun. Just then the soul of John Wieners stood beside us and when he picked up the Burger King crown and set it on his courtly brow, you could see that it wasn't paper at all, but the live body of a blue claw crab, its shell delicately balancing on top of John's bald spot, its legs in the air like a Boston prostitute, and in each of its needley pincers a birthday candle glowing in the blue smoke of the Virgin Mary's cigarette.

in memory of John Wieners

TELL ON YOU

I. For a Cowper snow globe

Like shooting turkeys in a barrel, said the road, who didn't know a lick of
vernacular, or had become it, a field filling with loosestrife. Expectation outweighs
desire for most of a life. Here is the body filled with fluids, lifegiving and baneful,
draped in high-gloss advertisements for bra and panties, all shiny and clean from
chemicals like a pharmaceutical, or the more remanded form of men's drawers and
T-shirts made from natural cotton fibers, treated and bleached, threading your eyes
and mind to the pages of the Sunday *New York Times Magazine*; or expectation
wired to its own weight in knowledge and memory, black-and-white ads for
lingerie in *The Boston Globe.*

The plasma of things doesn't know me very well, does it?   Blank, gray squibs of sky seep through the dutchments of my body – "sky" or "time" or time's sky or its story that includes me now and then as always.   Thank God it doesn't know its own strength or I'd be crushed under the stony ground after it pulled out all my hair in clumps and let me cast no shadow anymore, motioning with one arm to cross the street while with the other arm a crossing guard makes a line of cars wait for me.

Here's what we mean by life: all the rules are rescinded except the ones that keep things standing, and it's bigger and whip-like, uncoiling with a snap that flicks the quivering cigarette out of the lovely actress's mouth so she can go back to licking and being licked. Sometimes it just slides in and out like a mink through the boards at the base of a barn wet with snow melt. Here's what we mean by life: I want to be the street. Because some things are immortal in keeping with the personal, it offers each one more access to the rest. It tells each beading mystery with chalky fingers.

If it's all the same to you, I might "shed" some tears, which is the language for Gore-Tex apparel whose porous, miraculous weaving sheds rain and snow while letting your own natural moisture, your sweating armpits and back, your crotch and buttocks, return their prayerful wetness to the environment which gave them life and which we should protect at all costs: where else can we turn, foretold or ordained or probable, given the laws, the carbon-fiber length and duration, the humid, diffuse ichor?

The soul is a carved wood napkin ring in the center of your chest. There is a complex system or network, a web of tubing designed to support the body around it. The soul is separated from capillary action, which is a theorem of the body smartly agreed to by the fathers of the church, whose portraits rest above a cloud-filled, absent base. The ring is pitted and worn from toxins which gravitate toward all living things like revenuers to moonshine in a backwoods still. There is a needle-thin sliver of soap about to evaporate at the edge of the bathroom drain which is your soul.

Today's rain will be played by its understudy. My address book has some passages that are read over and over, some are called less frequently but are still important (some "vitally" important), and some are mere narrative tissue connecting the sung parts. The address book is the most published book in the history of the world – not the Bible as is commonly believed – and its blank pages are written by the reader. You buy the book and then author it, at first with careful attention to detail and editing, but mine is now so stuffed with the text of my life that I have to put new numbers under Z without any ordering principle except time and memory: now where did I put that number? not in D; then I remember, the back pages of Z, running a finger pointing out of need or desire down the names in my book of life. Memory and placement and feel. Indexing is a species of madness. "Time" and "time passing" or time's story only "lives with" history, then scuttles away like those little green crabs living under the rocks at the beach which I could snatch up in my closed fist with one shot like a god and feel their needley legs and their pincer jaws not even able to pierce the epidermis of my hand dripping with salt water.

A young woman, a girl not half my age, waiting across the street for the light to change, wearing extra-wide bell bottoms that used to be the fashion, each pant leg so wide and ocean blue – the ocean which is more than twice my age – each pant leg swirling like a blue emulsion added to the transparent beaker of day as she steps off the curb when the WALK sign comes on, lanes of traffic now empty as if the tide had suddenly gone out, the immediate transition, FedExing of time that we understand to be the case, grammar of distant things and things that are near, dim sliding cone to be "with" and "of" – for the young woman perhaps *along* the linings of the heart, in the middle of the chest, beating with linnet wings like a syringe.

Standing on the sidewalk grating above the subway when a train pulls in like all the pots and pans that had been asleep on a kitchen shelf or hanging bat-like on the wall crashed to the floor, bouncing off the stove top, all the mechanical milling and mining ripping ore out of the earth which gave it birth, the grinding and shrieking of tooling machines absorbed by these domestic wares, stored up inside them, released from the ground beneath my feet like in a movie when the music is saying you are getting a little bit closer to the secret thing the story knows.

The decade of school recess, the decade of physics used to murder, the decade of half-wished for things, the decade of squid, the decade of heart and facial cream, the silent decade of Jantzen swimwear, the decade of informal red-leather pants, the decade that cooed because it was pigeon-toed, the decade that couldn't pronounce the last syllable of recorded time right before the decade that ate all of its chocolate bars, the decade of Sir Walter Raleigh, the decade of the tip of the plume in Sir Walter Raleigh's hat to which no poem has ever been dedicated, the last decade of Sir Walter Raleigh's mammy, the decade of the lullabies he whispered under his breath when he slaughtered the Irish, the decades of the rosary they prayed when he was coming, the decade lost in space, the decade neck and the decade heart, the decade between your legs.

Do you see the running jump? I think we can make it. I think we can make it through the night, goes the lymph gland under my arm. I mean, this is a lyric of a popular song from the 80's, minus the gland. I think we can take the cusp and this is February. I think there is a panic in my tubing. The sun presents its fission of heaven, the vibration of nice things and the vibration of bad things interact on earth giving us a taste for a vibrating subset of these things. The wavy lime-colored lines on a hospital monitor where *We perish'd, each alone* could be engraved – here, let me give it a good shake like a snow globe and watch the shimmering green and radiant flakes float down.

Robert Stein

HAPPINESS

The unpierced sky. The bay with the broken ship.
The silver-frosted ground where we could not dig.
The day when I threw my ball up and it didn't come back.
My mother and this man forgetting my birthday.

When I fell over again it was ECT.
(*Easy tea* Jack grinned and called it).
The expensive shiny machine just for me –
Thump, *Mary God!* Mary and all the saints cracking my red heart, ecstasy!

THE DISCIPLES

Have had enough of this. They've all gone swimming.
It is a hot day, everyone is naked and some women have joined them.
With their clothes they've taken off fear & memories, nationhood & blood.
Their bodies move slowly in the water. They move slowly like clouds.
They rip the water over each other in joy.
The water-spits are, in a blink, haloes there.
They sit, after swimming, and eat and drink.
Nothing lies upon them but the water.

*

Tomorrow, or the next day, they will climb the old hill, pathless, laughing.
They will dance, or run. They will be friends or not friends.
Some will go up to the very top and lean themselves like white flags in the wind.
They will open their mouths newly and the sun will sing.

Essays

RICHARD PRICE

Generosity

So while you've this passion for leek vinaigrette,
you know what it means – no French kissing yet.

(Martial, Book XIII (*Xenia*), xviii, translated by Hamish Whyte)

"XENIA" DERIVES FROM an ancient Greek word which some dictionaries translate as "strange" and some as "hospitality". The Romans borrowed the term: it refers to little poems attached to objects that guests were given to take away with them, probably after a dinner party. It's a tradition similar to the practice today of party bags, those little bags containing sweets and perhaps an inexpensive toy given to children as they leave at the close of a celebration. The singular is "xenion", the xenion above referring to a gift of leeks.

The same source is most encountered in English, perhaps typically, within a negative compound, "xenophobia". Although xenophobia is usually described as the fear and hatred of foreigners and the foreign, the question mark in its etymology suggests something more complex, something meaner, something rather more close to home than that. Its modern-day usage is surely conditioned by an aversion to hospitality as much as to the foreign, an aversion to active goodwill, to trust, an aversion to the risk that any act of generosity must always entail.

I think immediately of the *Daily Mail* when I think of English xenophobia. Wrongly, because I know that *Daily Mail* readers – people like anyone else, if I may risk condescension in so saying – should not have their identities circumscribed by an easy interpretation of any one behavioural trait, not least the profoundly ambiguous act of reading one publication.

And, after all, no British newspaper is immune to a tone at odds with civil discourse. The *Independent* and the *Guardian*, papers which are sometimes, however rashly, taken to represent ground on the middle or even the left of the political spectrum (producing stories that are coterminous with a rational presentation of information) aren't above the constraints of their form. They have more information, and they have more sophisticated ways of being responsive to their own mistakes, but many readers will find these papers, too, read at times discordantly: in their case, like the mouthpiece of any loyal subject born and bred in the ancient villages of Toldyouçeaux or Tooclever-by-Half.

The larger audiences for the broadcast media make theirs, if anything, a more serious case. The BBC may claim to be unbiased, but anyone who has watched their "24 hour news" TV channel and seen the same half dozen pat stories recycled like bad air across the hour and throughout the day, will know that they are far from being comprehensive, especially at the point when they claim most to be. The gaps themselves point to a structural prejudice. The world is full of content, but BBC "Worldwide" appears to exist in a near-vacuum.

Why is this? And why raise it in an essay about poetry, about generosity?

It's a question of informational form, of having to add half-story to half-story, while leaving so many full stories completely out. Because it's actually very difficult to write news within the rules of what news must be – a particular kind of brevity is only one constraint, a particular kind of prosody, "topicality", "an angle", and "public interest" are others – without failing the spirit of truth, if not its letter. Often, its letter, too.

Many readers of poetry, though not exclusively readers of poetry (let's not get carried away with ourselves, here), will recognise this immediately. Poetry, by and large, won't actually tell a reader much that is factually new. Pound was saying this when he seemed not to be saying it in his phrase "Poetry is news that stays news". A formal knowledge of such a rich and technically nuanced medium as poetry, will engender a sensitivity to the technical limitations of any text, the way in which words serve the characteristics of each particular genre, and what a slave truth is to the conventions of each and every mode of communication. This doesn't mean that "everything is relative" or that "there's no such thing as truth", phrases which take the worst-case scenario as if it were the norm. It does mean, though, that one or two steps have to be taken to get round the particular kind of pre-processing of information the print and broadcast media represent.

Of course, readers may always have to turn to newspapers and the online and broadcast services for some recent information, but if they are alive to the formal qualities of the news story (which means being alive to the formal deficiencies, too), they will know they will have to look in other places as well. This is exactly the same as not accepting the four or five well-known poetry imprints as *necessarily* hallmarks of quality: no reader of poetry could seriously believe that these are guarantors of the best, even though the reader knows he or she may have to work hard to find alternatives.

In the world of news, to correct, re-orientate, and downgrade such mainstream sources, readers will need to read single-issue sites, say, and tap in to information networks less directly mediated by what are taken to be commercial and state imperatives; they'll have, at times, to consult genuine (as opposed to cuttings) libraries, whose careful memories often contradict the instant histories used by the media; and, perhaps as important as anything else, they'll have to enjoy the conversation of friends good enough to refine the arguments of each other and contradict each other's prejudices.

Friends aren't always easy to find, but more formalised circles – be it book groups, poetry workshops, or support or action groups, all of which, in themselves, may have nothing to do with ideas of a more generalised engagement with the mediators of power – may all provide the grounds for developing a means of social scrutiny that can be transferred and bring life back to the larger power structures and institutions, if they are found to be worth saving.

Animated discussion with those you love is one of the great pleasures, and xenia are surely presented in the same spirit. Open conversation may not always have been possible at the parties where xenia were given, but I like to think that some meetings would have been among trusted friends only, and then relaxed conversation would have gone on for hours. To folk who prefer the noun "crony" to the noun "friend", it is easy to traduce talk like that as "chattering", but, political insider-trading notwithstanding, everyone, I hope, can rise above the jagged naming words of media expressionism. The generosity of relaxed conversation is one of humanity's great "gifts", and I see xenia as symbolising a more intimate variation on the evening's group conviviality, a host's letting each guest know that they have all been thought of individually, too.

Each poem would be epigrammatic in character, and would, ideally, say something witty

about the gift and the host's relationship to the guest. It might affectionately refer to one of the guest's traits. Martial's *Apophoreta*, strictly speaking a more impersonal form of label, since the term refers to inscriptions for gifts that might well be drawn by lots at the party, seem occasionally to have this sense of intimacy, too:

> So take this torch to light your way at night:
> It's shockproof, like my heart, and weathertight.

> (Martial, Book XIV (*Apophoreta*), lxi. From *Martial Mottoes*,
> translated by Hamish Whyte, Galdragon Press, 1998)

Here, perhaps the guest had talked on a previous occasion about the long unlit pathway to his or her villa; perhaps they had said they'd been having nightmares in their new house, or they'd mentioned how dark the rooms were, even in summer. The torch, modernised by Whyte to suggest both actual and emotional electricity, has therefore become an attentive kindness and a joke between them, and there is clearly some romantic "charge" between giver and receiver, too. My speculations are another way of saying that there is some contextual secrecy in this poem, the sort of secrecy inherent in any intimacy, romantic or otherwise. That privacy is not a danger to the poem once it has been accepted as an element of it, and, as with any poem, especially poems that are far more opaque than this one, readers should not run to be excluded by something they think they don't immediately understand. The reader has to be generous to the poem so that it can be generous to the reader.

By having these apparently private poems published, Martial allowed them a public role. He gifted them beyond the individualism normally implied by the idea of the gift: he encouraged their enjoyment and interpretation beyond the specifics of their occasion. Xenia and apophoreta were witty, even edgy at times, and Martial is seldom remembered without a recollection of his sharp tongue. I hope I don't overstate the case for his work's gregariousness, although accusatory wit is also an acceptance of a social world where satire has force. If the giver acts indiscriminately, showering gifts on one person, say, or giving to all, generosity must be devalued. As long as mean-spiritedness is not involved, generosity actually needs a critical intelligence, even a kind of hardness, to keep its worth.

At xenia parties, maybe gift and poem were used ostentatiously: you can imagine the tagged presents stacked in a specially prepared corner in the room the host had chosen for the party. They could even be presented one by one to those in attendance as part of the proceedings. Martial structures his book of xenia to correspond to the courses of the Roman dinner, so a variation on the reading of Christmas cracker mottoes comes to mind, with or without the groans at awful jokes. Performance, banter and fun: all the senses and the near-perfection of the best parties.

(Yet some hosts, I'm sure, would have preferred to be more discreet, maybe keeping the treats out of sight until the end of the evening when they'd be handed to each guest as good-byes and a special word or two would be said.)

When Hamish Whyte offers two of his translations as gifts in themselves, in a *festschrift* to the poet Gael Turnbull on the occasion of his seventieth birthday, this complex private/public package of the epigram tradition is picked up and passed on, pass-the-parcel style, as much to new readers of Turnbull as to the esteemed poet himself. The first, in particular, is a kind of non-gift gift. It names something of which Gael Turnbull had better not be the recipient: dumb-bells. Metonymic "vineyards" (bearing poetic fruit) are appropriately to the fore:

"Dumb-bells"

Leave the dumb dumb-bells to the chaps at the gym –
trenching vineyards will keep you in better trim.

(Martial, translated by Hamish Whyte, Book XIV (*Apophoreta*), xlix.
Taken from *A Gathering for Gael Turnbull*, ed. Peter McCarey, Au Quai, 1998)

Martial has been put to much denser use, too. Arkadii Dragomoschenko's long poem, called *Xenia*, in the translation by Lyn Hejinian and Elena Balashova, remembers a present as a means of making a momentary ascent through an unbreathable medium that might be memory itself – "You rip off the gift's waxed string and you follow the ascent / of the oxygen bubbles". I think of Orson Welles's sledge *Rosebud* here, a present that joins childhood to the dying hero's last moments, and I think of the way Eugenio Montale modernises the epigram tradition, too, in the "Xenia" sequences in his late work *Satura*. Here there is less comfort: the "gifts" are actually the last points of contact between the dead and the living. Material ephemera, the individual objects of all our clutter, offer surprisingly plangent effects: a little thing like the label on a bottle of wine or a now much diminished phone bill, becomes unexpectedly an elegiac remembrance of Montale's late wife. What the gift, what generosity is, shifts and almost evades us: presents always end up conventionally useless, but they become, ideally, tags to the real gifts, the memories to which they, and we, have become so attached.

Xenia have a distant relative in Anglo-Saxon riddles, where the focus was, again, on the beauty and mystery of humble and familiar objects. Riddles, however, defer pleasure: they tease and puzzle, and they make very strange the familiar. The familiar can be made so strange, in fact, that some of the riddles in the main repository of Anglo-Saxon riddles, the *Exeter Book*, have today no secure solution.

For instance there's Riddle 90, which begins, "A strange thing it seemed to me / a wolf captured by a lamb". "The lamb lay down by a rock, / and pull[ed] out the wolf's bowels" it goes on (the Anglo-Saxons had a rather closer relationship to animals than most in the West have now), before ending "I saw a great marvel, / two wolves standing tormenting a third; / they had four feet, they saw with seven eyes." (John Porter, translator, *Anglo-Saxon Riddles*, Anglo-Saxon Books, 1995).

Any answers?

A table and some points of light? Candles, jewels? The lamb might suggest Christian resonances since, though most are secular, one or two of the riddles are biblical. I'm afraid I can offer nothing better than that, but the idea of such a long unsolved riddle makes me smile. I guess it was solved at a point closer to the time it was written, only to be forgotten later on.

Sometimes a poem that works in a way with which the reader is not immediately familiar is accused of being like a crossword puzzle. I think it was Norman MacCaig who recalled how one of the readers of his early New Apocalypse verse wrote to him in perplexity, expressing the hope that the poet would one day publish the answers. Yet even with the enigma of Riddle 90, where there really is a particular subject that has been deliberately disguised, the poem does not need that meaning to show a good deal of its beauty.

It is almost shocking, but it is beautiful nevertheless, and the poem has a skilled alliterative musicality in the original. These are the "gift" elements of a poem that was most likely intended more as a challenge, and as a piece of public virtuosity, but whose rhythmic, structural, and nuanced sound qualities cannot help but give pleasure.

For those who try to understand "difficult poems", some of which really aren't about decoding one text into a clearer shorter one, into some "real message" or "solution" (imagine listening to songs that way! What would be the point?), such a riddle offers an oblique lesson. The "poemy" aspects can be the greater part of opaque poems. Not, as sometimes they're taken to be, "a private world". Not, in fact, "too personal" to be understood, not "too academic". Rather, poems experienced by readers or listeners almost as they might experience a piece of music or a painting which they cannot wholly accommodate within the sense-making world of their previous experience. People find one or two points that they can fix on – perhaps they like the rhythm or the hook in a song without really knowing what it's all about, or the balance of colour in a painting – and then they live with it, hear it again, take another look, never thinking for a moment that they will understand it all or, just as importantly, that there is necessarily a single overarching thing to be understood. They are already relaxed enough to begin to enjoy themselves (taking "enjoyment" to include a range of emotions: contemplation, much smiling, pretending to be appalled, etc).

Some of my most important reading experiences have been through being encouraged to relax with a poet's work in this way. Friends' recommendations that I read, say, Denise Riley, or Kelvin Corcoran, or, more recently, Karlien van den Beukel, have modified my whole reading and writing practice, have simply allowed me to be in the company of kinds of pleasure and articulacy that, good literary criticism notwithstanding, I might well not have otherwise encountered.

I don't deny that there may be some "health-giving" corporal punishment in the minds of some "difficult" poets, but instead of treating their poems as an ordeal that the poet hopes will be good for its reader in the long run, it's maybe better, whatever it is felt the poet's intentions are, to see such work as a *gift* to the reader, as an act of generosity, as something which can be domesticated in whatever way the reader and the text can agree on, and lived with in that way. I'm not expressing an attitude of "anything goes": rather I'm suggesting an evidence-based faith ("evidence-based faith" is, after all, a definition of science) in the ability of the "poemy" cues in a poem to offer up pleasure and other shades of feeling, as well as the points of interest that more straightforward, if less poemy, poems offer.

Generosity is always difficult, in fact. Biological case studies show powerful gift-giving urges in many species, often but not exclusively associated with sexual impulses. For the recipient, gifts can be very mysterious things indeed. I think of the track "A hymn for the postal service" on Hefner's album *Breaking God's heart*. (Hefner are in the post-punk tradition of The Buzzcocks, whose "Ever fallen in love with someone you shouldn't have fallen in love with?" still resonates, to me, as one of the simplest and best songs of the past quarter century.) In "A hymn" there is that familiar sense of being in the throes of enslaving emotions, but the pace is slower, the narrative more complicated. The singer's object of desire, Lydia Pond, has moved to Paris to get away from British politics. There she sends back a passport photo of herself in pigtails and, to the singer's frustration and puzzlement, her letters "used the f-word / when she never ever spoke it". Here the gift – a letter between friends, not to mention lovers, is always a gift – becomes a sexual and social mystery. Is

Lydia Pond teasing the singer? Does her swearing on paper suggest a new intimacy – either a lover's intimacy where next to nothing is barred, or, to the singer, merely a friend's intimacy (since some kinds of lovers' relationships may force each to be on their swearless best behaviour)? Do the swear words suggest the promise of desire's ultimate closeness or friendship's ultimate distance? She promises him "they'll be creasing sheets", but a strong tone within the song is one of unluckiness, of the singer's failure and bewilderment. In the end the singer describes becoming faithful, not to Lydia, but to her letters: the gift has become not intermediary but object of desire.

What is so ambiguous and tension-making about gifts actually contributes to their definition. The doubts and hints and selectivity, the half-obligations, the danger of giving too little and "being cheap", or of giving too much: the impurities of the gift transaction, its snaggish social qualities, are critical to the sense of what gift is.

A gift given to a hoped-for lover, for instance, takes the risk that the loved one may not at all like this *particular* thing. Except for ironic purposes, it mustn't be an anodyne, generic gift that anyone would think "nice" or "dutiful". It must be specific to the person and so well-thought-out (but preferably not agonised over, preferably *as if* spontaneous), and it must, to some degree, confirm the receiver's own self-image without duplicating an item the receiver already has. How far from that self-image the gift may be is a fine judgement, and a judgement made in different ways for different lovers, since a gift ideally should represent something of what the giver takes to be important to him or herself: there is development and movement and progress in that, and it is in this field of risky generosity that poems, those special gifts, best belong.

The Baby and the Bathwater – Lawrence, Poetry and Class

DAVID ELLIS

IN THE POEMS Lawrence wrote in the last two years of his life – the ones he called pansies because, as Ophelia says, "And there is pansies, that's for thoughts" – there is a good deal of class feeling. The much anthologised "The Oxford Voice" is no more a compliment to its subject than "How Beastly the Bourgeois is" and several other pansies are of the same type. In "Red-Herring" Lawrence chose a ballad form to reflect on his own social background.

> My father was a working man
>   and a collier was he,
> at six in the morning they turned him down
>   and they turned him up for tea.
>
> My mother was a superior soul
>   a superior soul was she,
> cut out to play a superior role
>   in the god-damn bourgeoisie.

> We children were the in-betweens
> little non-descripts were we,
> indoors we called each other *you*,
> outside, it was *tha* and *thee*.

A mother's boy if ever there was one, Lawrence was responsive in his early days to her desire that all her children should escape their proletarian environment and become members of the middle class, that they should "get on". But as he grew older, and became more acutely conscious of the anomalies of his situation, he tended to side with his father and feel nostalgia for the way of life he represented.

Lawrence's class background had important implications for his efforts to become a writer. He began with poetry, but must have been uncomfortably aware that writing poems was hardly a common occupation for a miner's son. Certainly he was self-conscious and secretive about his work and made no effort to have it published. It was his close friend Jessie Chambers who, in 1909, collected together a number of pieces and sent them to Ford Maddox Hueffer's *English Review*. Lawrence's early verse is over-elaborate and affected, full of echoes of the pre-Raphaelites and other post-Romantics. The work of any young poet of his time is likely to have been derivative in a similar way, but there were special complications for Lawrence in his struggle to adapt for his own purposes the poetic idiom which was then in fashion. Brought up a bilingual, his aspirations to be "literary" must have been hard to distinguish from the desire his mother had instilled in him to be middle-class.

There is every likelihood that one of the reasons Hueffer accepted the poems Jessie Chambers sent to him was that he was aware of their author's social origins. He took Lawrence up, introducing him to literary London so that, while he was still an elementary schoolmaster in Croydon, he attended gatherings where Yeats read his poetry and where he met Ezra Pound. Lawrence understood the English class system too well not to know that he could hardly enjoy these unexpected advantages without being patronised from time to time. She was "really so strongly entrenched in her class superiority", he writes of Hermione Roddice in *Women in Love*, that "she could come up and know people out of simple curiosity, as if they were creatures on exhibition". Hueffer, however, he always remembered warmly – "the first man I ever met who had a real and true feeling for literature" - and he claimed to have been merely amused when Hueffer shouted to him on a bus "But you've got GENIUS" (the "but" was crucial). "This made me want to laugh", he wrote, "it sounded so comical. In the early days they were always telling me I had got genius, as if to console me for not having their own incomparable advantages". Despite Nottingham High School and a year at Nottingham University, the image of a talented but uneducated writer, warbling his native wood-notes wild, was one which Lawrence had to cope with all his life.

At the time of his first contacts with literary London, Lawrence was writing a novel in which elements of his own early experience were transposed into a genteel, middle-class environment (it eventually became *The White Peacock*). As John Worthen has pointed out, Hueffer was on the lookout for writers who could describe working-class life and it may therefore have been no coincidence that only shortly after first meeting him Lawrence wrote his short story "Odour of Chrysanthemums", that minor tragedy of mining life, and his first play, *A Collier's Friday Night*. Since in both these works confident familiarity with the material he is handling appears to bring with it a sparer, more direct idiom, the influence of Hueffer can only be described as positive, at least as far as prose fiction and drama were concerned. The situation regarding Lawrence's poetry was more complicated. It is unlikely, for example, that he would have been entirely happy with the way Pound reviewed his first volume of poems, *Love Poems and Others*, published in 1913. If by love poems, Pound wrote, Lawrence meant "the middling-sensual erotic verses in this collection", then they are "a sort of pre-raphaelitish slush, disgusting or very nearly so". However, "when Mr Lawrence ceases to discuss his own disagreeable sensations, when he writes low-life narrative, as he does in 'Whether or Not' and in 'Violets', there is no English poet under forty who can get within a shot of him". The two poems Pound mentions are in dialect, and since they benefit from Lawrence's highly developed dramatic sense, and his acute ear for dialogue, they may well be the best poems in the volume. But in praising them as he does, Pound implicitly condemns Lawrence to remaining a curiosity, the working-class recorder of strange working-class rituals, and patronisingly dismisses his efforts to find an appropriate language for his "disagreeable sensations". Yet those sensations were vitally important to him, and he was not going to be put off by Pound from trying to develop a voice in which he could express them effectively.

Lawrence always spoke with a regional accent, but in England it is not only region which is betrayed by the way we speak. Why go to the bother of introducing identity cards when, for the acute, instinctively discriminating listeners English people are, we already carry them in our vowels? Once he had met Frieda von Richthofen, the woman who would become his wife, Lawrence lived abroad whenever he could, enjoying that liberation which comes from being virtually incognito. To be broadly stereo-typed as "English" by foreigners can be easier to bear than the close identifications and pigeonholing of compatriots. Class must have had a part to play in all his life decisions, and it also helps to explain why it was not an English but an American poet who most helped him to find his own poetic voice. This was not, of course, Pound but Whitman. Lawrence made his debt to Whitman explicit in his introduction to the 1918 American edition of his *New Poems* (scraped together in hard times and not, in fact, at all new). The discovery of Whitman's "free verse" was a liberation for Lawrence analogous to that of living abroad, and he makes clear in his introduction that there was much more involved than metre.

> Free verse toes no melodic line, no matter what drill-sergeant. Whitman pruned away his clichés – perhaps his clichés of rhythm as well as of phrase. And this is about all we can do, deliberately, with free verse. We can get rid of the stereotyped movements and the old hackneyed associations of sound or sense. We can break down those artificial conduits and canals through which we do so love to force our utterance.

Frieda had a lot to do with ridding Lawrence's verse of its pretensions, another significant contributory factor was the misery he suffered during the First World War, but, as far as literary models are concerned, it was above all the foreign voice of Whitman which showed him how it was possible to write poetry which was not "poetic".

The beneficial effects of Whitman's example are first clearly evident in *Look! We Have Come Through!* (1917). Most of the poems in this collection record the tortuous progress of Lawrence's relations with his wife, and have therefore been felt by many readers to involve sensations which are "disagreeable", or at least uncomfortably intimate. They have preferred the next volume which consists of poems most of which ("Peach", "Man and Bat", "Snake", the tortoise sequence) were written in Italy in 1921. These often also deal with the painful aspects of relations between men and women, but at several removes and through the intermediary of vivid descriptions of the natural world: animal, vegetable, or even mineral. The voice in these poems is like a stream run clear: direct, adaptable and free of self-consciousness, for all seasons and for all classes. It is paradoxical that just as Lawrence achieves this ease and assurance in his poetry, the voice in his fiction becomes uncertain and, in the case of *Mr Noon* especially, full of awkward ironic addresses to a "gentle reader" who is quickly made to feel that he or she is not gentle at all. This was because, after the suppression of *The Rainbow*, and the difficulties he then experienced in getting *Women in Love* into print, Lawrence had begun to wonder whether he had any kind of public and where he could find any reasonably sympathetic audience. When he wrote poems, on the other hand, the question of his readers seemed to have been far from his mind, either because he did not expect to have many, or because he felt that they would be of a different kind from those who read his novels.

> Mellors is, after all, precisely the "in-between" Lawrence felt he himself had become, someone able to operate successfully in a middle-class world but never fully accepted by it; attracted to working-class values yet unable to make his own life among working-class people

After *Birds, Beasts and Flowers* Lawrence wrote scarcely any poetry until his publisher suggested he should prepare an edition of his *Collected Poems* (1928). Assembling and re-reading his early verse must have brought back the miseries of his early emotional entanglements, and it certainly made him feel dissatisfied with the manner in which they had been expressed. It was, therefore, through re-writing a good deal of his early work that he came back to poetry, although it is also true that, as he became increasingly ill and obliged to spend more of each day in bed, a short poem began to represent a more manageable form of complete self-expression than even the shortest prose fiction. It meant he could have his say without having to worry what the next day would bring.

Revisiting his youth through his early verse must also have been one of the many factors which contributed to that welling-up of class feeling so apparent in his last years. Retrospection brings us clearer understanding of what once made us happy or miserable, and although Lawrence was, by our standards, a comparatively young man when he began reviewing his previous life, he was also a very sick one. From 1919 until his death in 1930 he lived abroad, making only three short trips back to England. The last of these, in 1926, coincided with the General Strike so that he was visiting his old haunts in the Midlands, and meeting some of the people he had known in his youth, at a time when the deep divisions of English society were more openly acknowledged than they had been for a long time. He used memories of this last trip for the setting of *Lady Chatterley's Lover*, the prose work in which the bitterness of his class feeling is most clear and urgent. Mellors is, after all, precisely the "in-between" Lawrence felt he himself had become, someone able to operate successfully in a middle-class world but never fully accepted by it; attracted to working-class values yet unable to make his own life among working-class people.

There are obvious connections between Mellors and "The Oxford Voice" or "How Beastly the Bourgeois Is" (he might have written both), as there are between class resentments and antagonisms in *Lady Chatterley's Lover* and the feeling about social

relations in England which pervades all the pansies (including those Aldington called "last poems"). Some critics have felt that it is class feeling which, even more than sexual explicitness, makes the novel so unpleasant (in the scene, for example, in which Mellors uses his ability to talk dialect as a weapon against Connie's sister Hilda), but the query raised by the two poems I mention, or by "Red-Herring", is rather whether they qualify as poetry at all. Certainly they show ease and assurance, an ability to manipulate different verse forms, but in ridding his verse of affectation and no longer striving to be poetic, might not Lawrence have permanently thrown the baby out with the bath water? The degree of his assurance is evident in a pansy such as "Leda":

> Come not with kisses
> not with caresses
> of hands and lips and murmurings;
> come with a hiss of wings
> and sea-touch tip of a beak
> and treading of wet, webbed, wave-working feet
> into the marsh-soft belly.

This is surely a remarkable *poem*. Swans stimulated Lawrence's imagination in a highly distinctive, un-Yeatsean way. But it needs a longer piece to show how he was able to combine the lyrical impulse of "Leda" with the satirical note so evident in the complaints he makes against the English class system elsewhere in his pansies. Consider for instance:

> Won't it be strange, when the nurse brings the new-born infant
> to the proud father, and shows its little, webbed greenish feet
> made to smite the waters behind it?
> or the round, wild vivid eye of a wild-goose staring
> out of fathomless skies and seas?
> or when he utters that undaunted little bird-cry
> of one who will settle on ice-bergs, and honk across the Nile?
>
> And when the father says: This is none of mine!
> Woman, where got you this little beast?
> will there be a whistle of wings in the air, and an icy draught?
> will the singing of swans, high up, high up, invisible
> break the drums of his ears
> and leave him forever listening for the answer?

By no means all the pansies are of this quality, but as Dr Johnson said of Pope's work, if this is not poetry, where is poetry to be found?

Class played an important and determining role in Lawrence's development as a writer. Although his experience during the First World War was the principal cause for the alienation and bitterness he experienced in his life-time, and for the self-imposed isolation in which he chiefly lived during the 1920s, his social origins had made him an outsider before the war began. Something of what he had to deal with is suggested by David Garnett's account of first meeting Lawrence in 1912. "His hair", Garnett wrote, "was of a colour, and grew in a particular way, which I have never seen except in English working men. It was bright mud-colour, with a streak of red in it, a thick mat, parted on one side. Somehow, it was incredibly plebeian, mongrel and underbred . . . . He was the weedy runt you find in every gang of workmen: the one who keeps the other men laughing all the time; who makes trouble with the boss and is saucy to the foreman". It is hard to be fixed in the mind of a quite significant other in this way even *before* you have opened your mouth.

How much class continued to matter after Lawrence's time, and still matters, are open questions. To at least the first of them, one writer, whose career in many ways mirrors that of Lawrence, and whose recent death at the very end of last year was such a blow to anyone who cares about poetry, would have had a ready answer. D. J. Enright was brought up in a working-class household in Leamington, went on to university and then, like Lawrence, spent much of his life abroad. In *The Terrible Shears: Scenes from a Twenties Childhood* he vividly evokes his upbringing through a series of vignettes many of which manage to be both comic and touching. One of them has "Class" as its title:

> I can't help it, I still get mad
> When people say that "class" doesn't mean
> A thing, and to mention one's working-class
> Origins is "inverted snobbery".
>
> The wife of a teacher at school (she was
> Mother of one of my classmates) was
> Genuinely enraged when I won a scholarship.
> She stopped me in the street, to tell me
> (With a loudness I supposed was upper-class)
> That Cambridge was not for the likes of me, nor was
> Long hair, nor the verse I wrote for the school mag.
>
> Her sentiments were precisely those of the
> Working class. Unanimity on basic questions
> Accounts for why we never had the revolution.

Like much of Enright's later work, this poem has the directness and simplicity of Lawrence's pansies, although also his own characteristic sardonic humour. ("We had to keep our coal out at the back", the first poem in *The Terrible Shears* memorably begins, "They wouldn't give us a bath".) That humour is necessary to avoid the charge of trading on one's origins which became common after Lawrence's time, and which is implicit in the reference to "inverted snobbery". Simple as it appears, the poem makes a subtle distinction between the boy who supposes the woman to be upper class and the mature writer who, however much he resents class prejudice, knows that it would be false to imply that he ever was or could ever be completely at one with its victims. That is because the working class writer, even at the stage where his only outlet is the school magazine, is fated to be what in "Red Herring" Lawrence calls an "in-between". Writers are of necessity, or by vocation, solitary creatures, difficult to fit into any social system, but there is nonetheless a bond which comes from doing more or less the same kind of work as other people. In the England of the past, however, the links forged by a common activity seem often in their case to have been less strong than those which depended on having had a similar social background. What a mercy it would indeed be if we now have (as the French are supposed to say) changed all that.

Reviews

Disobeying Orders

ROBERT POTTS

Keston Sutherland, *Antifreeze*
Barque Press, £8.00, ISBN 1903488257
Keston Sutherland, *The Rictus Flag*
Object Permanence, £3.00 (incl. p&p in the UK), ISBN 1903488168
Keston Sutherland, editor, *Quid* magazine
£1.00 each, Barque Press

IN EARLY 2001, Barque Press published *100 Days*, an anthology of poems edited by Andrea Brady, responding to the first hundred days of the Bush administration. There are several things to note about it: first that it was a "rapid response", released with a sense of horrified urgency, in the manner of some recent anti-war anthologies: second, that it was a communal activity, the result of feelers sent out through the internet and across loosely interlinked communities of artists and writers; and third, that its level of informed anger is quite unusual for a British poetry anthology – everything about the Bush administration, from its links with oil and arms to its stance on abortion, *inter alia*, is considered, and an appendix itemises, blow by blow, day by day, the legislation and policy enacted even in the first few months after an election of "contested" legitimacy.

Barque Press is run by Brady herself and by Keston Sutherland: Sutherland also publishes the irregular magazine, *Quid*, which has, in the past few years, become a similarly fascinating intervention, offering poems, essays, politics, poetics, reviews, and polemics. The magazine is photocopied ("Xerox turned fiery gorge") and chunky, and though conceived of as a monthly publication is somewhat less frequent than that. It costs one pound, as its name suggests. You get a remarkable amount for your money – *Quid* #9, "Against Imperialism", is fifty pages long, for instance.

Recent and substantial essays and articles include Ben Watson and Esther Leslie's joint piece, "Write to Live; Live To Write: Trading ideas in academia and journalism"; Peter Middleton's essay "Dirigibles", which starts with the invention of speech bubbles in cartoons and develops, via sundry interesting thoughts, into an essay about interpretation as a communal activity; Andrea Brady's "Grief Work in a War Economy", in response to September 11; and Andrew Duncan explaining very clearly why (in early 2002) he would not write about Afghanistan:

> The minimum requirement for doing so would be an acquaintance with the main linguistic and ethnic cultures bundled up within the country. . . . Anything less is brushing the edges of depersonalization (people not allowed to be the subjects of their own history) and a cigarette-card approach (where all Afghans behave in the same way and we don't need to differentiate).

Instead, Duncan starts to explore the limits and uses of political knowledge and understanding, and startlingly remarks: "Is it absurd for a poet to have a foreign policy? My contention is that it is not".

Quid is also bold enough to contain genuinely critical responses to some of its contents; particularly two extended pieces by Peter Riley that ask pained and pointed questions about the sort of poetry produced by, well, the sort of poets published in *Quid*. That is to say, *Quid* is wide-ranging, left-wing, intelligent, unafraid of ideas, contemporary, and passionate. To buy 6, 7a, 7b, 7c, 8i, 8ii, 8iii, 9, 10i, 10ii, and 10iii, as I would recommend, would cost £11, plus post and packing.

Quid's other most striking pieces are Keston Sutherland's editorials; rapid, vivid excesses of language and passion, as if despair and idealism were twisting each other into new and peculiar shapes of dissent. His editorial on September 11 (and on the poetic response of the left) is impossible to quote without draining it of its ferocious energy: and Keith Tuma's response in the next issue was understandably tentative, but illuminatingly so –

> I found myself on a first reading waffling about how to take specific ironies . . . [his] alienation is manifest in an eloquence that eats itself . . . you will have to read the whole editorial to appreciate its virtuoso spin. Resignation and anger pushed past the point of explosion. There is a sick, unfair parallel one could outrageously venture: the use of homicidal suicide for political purposes.

Keston Sutherland as poetic suicide bomber? Tuma also describes Sutherland's approach as a "neglect of tactics": Sutherland responds "I do absolutely want to neglect tactics, though in the most positive and conscious manner only: to refuse them".

In his essays Sutherland turns certain assumptions about poetry on their heads. In "Bathos" (available online), he takes Pope's term for bad writing and puts it through a philosophical wringer to explore, *inter alia*, the political impotence of poetry, its awareness of that impotence, and his desire "to *feel* hope, and not only to desire it". In "Vagueness", the value traditionally placed on "precision" in poetry is errantly questioned. The essay, provokingly punctuated with the precise time at which it was being written ("This seems perhaps like an unfairly vague definition of history. It is. At 5.29 pm it is not looking any less unfair or vague, nor does it seem likely to become so . . ."), manages to discuss vagueness not only philosophically, but also poetically and politically. (At one point "clouds" as a Romantic symbol are related to the impact of meteorological conditions of precision-bombing raids.) It employs a series of manoeuvres that at times resemble those of a man who, having chained himself to a radiator, is now chewing through his own arm: "a kind of hypervigilance that baffles its own object" in Sutherland's own words. The essay ends: "Impossibility is not just a faded watchword echoing the 1960s campus occupations of 'Utopian' vocab. It is the absolute target-concept; it is a positive contingency of all humane expression . . . In poetry this impossible defiance shines, like love as an ideal-limit of hatred".

Sutherland was a student of J. H. Prynne's at Cambridge, and still lives and works in that city. (While there are traces of Prynne in his early writing, and some overt allusions, Sutherland is not, or no longer, easily placed by the label "Prynnite".) His poetry has a compelling musical energy; and there is also a persistent lyricism, however vexed and beleaguered. He is unafraid to use, at times, a sustained direct address, writing predominantly in the first person. Where he has most in common with some of the Cambridge poets and other avant-garde writers is his disruption of syntax:

> stops there and readies herself for conflict
>   resolution it says
> you picked that formalized modes of

arbitration, formalized modes of erotic happiness,
the star bangs you can think highly
across or sideways can an adduced fire thread
    they ask you
to envyless sedition, as the preferable
sun budges out, can it thread you to distort out
you're breaking up try no try okay
thread you to the panic of indefectible
    vanity, as in love the skyslide
impossible you are they
say . . .

Unfair, to quote out of context: nonetheless, one might immediately note the re-readings required by line breaks ("readies herself for conflict / resolution"), the eeriness of repetition (when the iterated "formalized modes" is brought incongruously, oxymoronically, up against "erotic happiness"), the way in which the poem is interfered with by other voices, notably the intrusive "they ask you" and "they say", but also the disruption by the fraught mobile phone dialogue – "you're breaking up try no try okay". Even presented with the apparent chaos of these lines from "The Little Match Girl", a reader cannot help registering these preliminary shapes within the noise.

In a recent *TLS*, the opera critic Andrew Porter quotes the composer Roger Sessions on "a listener's encounter with 'a new, unfamiliar, or difficult piece'":

> One's first impression may be a quite negative one; the music may seem opaque, chaotic, crabbed, dissonant . . . . But if we keep our ears open and willing, and listen attentively, we may easily discern, here and there, moments or passages of which we feel the impact immediately . . . . One may even tell oneself: "This at least is 'striking' – or 'graceful,' or 'amusing,' even 'moving,' 'beautiful,' or simply 'interesting.'" This means we have begun to recognize features in the work and to sense its character; and if we are interested or patient enough to pursue the matter further, we will find that these moments grow longer.

Given that Sutherland has been working in a milieu for whom his linguistic experiments are not wholly unprecedented, but has not been read much by those for whom any such experiments are "rebarbative", "difficult", "incomprehensible" and even "idiotic", a reviewer has a problem of address. Two distinct audiences emerge. The first audience will be aware of Sutherland's work, and will be primarily interested in exegetical and theoretical discussions of it. The latter audience will, most likely, not only not have heard of Sutherland, but will be initially highly uncomfortable with an unfamiliar reading experience. So it is this second audience to whom I want to write about Sutherland's work, and to whom I want to suggest "keeping our ears open and willing, and listening attentively". It is not just that "the moments become longer": this is a poetry that, instead of meeting our expectations and demands, consistently encourages us to change and exceed our expectations and demands, poetically and politically.

The speed and violence and intensity of Sutherland's poems is remarkable: they possess the velocity and energy of modern music, with its easy sampling of available fragments; and of modern cinema and video, with jumps, cuts, edits, and fades. (The titles – "Ritalin

Daiquiri", "Scunthorpe Mon Amour", "To the Last Ansaphone" – remind me of some of the better songs of The Fall.) To read them swiftly, as one does on a first encounter, is to be drawn in by their urgency while simultaneously buffeted by a welter of twisted images and broken phrases, disrupted syntax and bitten-off cries: line breaks force re-readings of words and phrases; repetitions add a propulsive rhythm to the process; shorter lines, indented interjections and stanza-breaks slow one down. There is a frequent use of catachresis – an impossible or inappropriate use of language. Gradually one finds the best speed at which to experience the poems' vitality and yet still to make efforts of interpretation; too slow and you'll lose the rush and the music, too fast and you experience the whole thing (wrongly) as a merely excited randomness. These torn and tearing pieces are contained in elegant and regular stanzaic shapes: there seems constantly a tug between order and disorder, with the tussle never resolved in either direction. That tussle is then experienced also by the reader.

Another feature, which differentiates it from certain other overtly experimental poetry, is the presence of some disarmingly direct emotional statements. Lucidity in the poems, though regular, seems always more shocking than one expects, as here, in "Ten Past Nine", where the bravado slides into attempted consolation and then moving abjection:

> In my speech shines a radiant energy,
> I can destroy hype, the wind flashes with its end,
> fury and barriers become smashed
> out, the music chars hype
> broke out from me. I sing and the serrated horizon
> tilts, dirt splashes become zero each. We are
> okay. I am not even a fucking person any more.

Many of the poems are love poems, though the nature and object of love can vary or be vague within the pieces; and when Sutherland writes about love or desire, the clarity with which statement emerges from the maelstrom is directly affecting and also haunting. (The erotic writing is also unsettlingly passionate and violent. "Raw" hardly does it justice.) Sutherland's poetry can seem very much like "the intelligence at bay", in those words of Pound which Geoffrey Hill loves to quote: but one equally experiences it as "desire at bay" – a passionate opposition to structures of injustice that erupt unavoidably into the poem, and are experienced viscerally and physically; affirmations of love squeezed through wreckage and despair.

So a poem like "Ode: What You Do" (published in *Poetry Review*, and available online) trembles between order and disorder. The poem is in five sections, each containing five three-line stanzas. Despite this order, "Ode" is a clearly disjointed text (syntactically it keeps breaking off: "this terrifying, and // correction, no-one"; "If you want to change the // tick alright"; "except that the – at first, I thought you / were crazy"; in other places the syntax seems almost absent: "It across-centre evocate at / snappy prolonged wind"). The disruption of word order and the ambiguity of pronouns call attention to exactly how far political ordering and division take place, as if naturally, in language: "Some / them are gay", for instance. One wants to read "some *of* them are gay", but it isn't that there is a clear category of "them", some of whom are gay; it is that dividing people by sexuality creates (for heterosexuals) a gay "them", a "not-us". In the earlier verses

                    If you want to change the

                    tick alright. Everyone's so – lymphatic
                    drainage from a primary lust for, tends
                    to, agrees with, makes a stab at,

                    wouldn't if you…

the ellipses and approximations do a number of things. The first line suggests an ambition ("change the world", is surely implied?) but eliminates the object of desire over the stanza break; the sentence resumes with a response inadequate to such ambitions: the mechanistic, consumer-society, faux-democratic "tick alright". "Everyone's so –" breaks off for the good reason that there is no truthful way to finish the colloquialism; it immediately reminds us of all the ways in which we might be specific and different rather than identical: which is why the initial misreading, "everyone's so lymphatic", is comic. "Tends to, agrees with, makes a stab at" is a phrase failing even to be precise about approximation.

Section 3 begins "Appropriate life is shredded in dreams / like soap in water. Dare to realize, and / weld forging of two, ask – get soapy // life mere twist into synecdoche, how you / stand for that." The mention of "synecdoche", another organizing trope in which part stands for whole or whole for part – "everyone's so" – is rounded off with a beautiful and protesting pun: "how you stand for that" is both a definition of synecdoche and a recog- nizable cry of disbelief: "how do you put up with this?"

Sutherland's work does make one unusually conscious of the potential effects of linguistic structures. Some of these are oppressive: it interests me that in these spare, apparently chaotic sentences, one hears so clearly the different intonations of scientific, personal, and bureaucratic language: when, as happens in several poems, the words "shut up" punctuate sentences, one hears a spitting violence; in "Deletes Sex" the mechanical instructions "edit", "cut", and suchlike punctuate the flow with impersonal brutality. In other places these re-orderings offer a greater sense of movement and possibility; Sutherland uses tmesis (the separation or splitting up of a word into parts by one or more intervening words, e.g. "abso-bloody-lutely"), as in "what uprearing assent soever" rather than "in whatsoever uprearing assent", and such tiny differences in the way in which one processes the line do make one construct and infer meaning differently before re-adjusting to the expected sense or senses.

At times this breaking of Subject-Verb-Object sentence construction, with verbs being held back, and qualifying clauses slipped in earlier than usual, is stunningly effective in setting up several possible outcomes at once, before the line flies off in another direction: it allows Sutherland to suggest, simultaneously, several mutually exclusive possibilities. While some of these are set up and implied by Sutherland's own choices and decisions, others will originate with the reader. The same applies to his use of oxymoron and catachresis: one is left with the ghost of the predictable phrase, superseded by the surreal or unreal way in which the line in fact continues.

And it strikes me that Sutherland's work attempts (in my view successfully) to explore, say, the individual's anger and impotence, and a larger set of political, economic, and tech- nological contexts, and the desire to transform those contexts, and the manners in which such desires are thwarted or attacked, and the exploration of possibilities of dissent and creative political change, and the pessimism that any such dissent is effectively impossible,

and more than this, *all at the same time.*

To describe it even in this way is hardly to do justice to work that has pushed itself so hard, theoretically, politically, existentially. And almost anything one says about it could be disputed by Sutherland, the refusenik's refusenik. When Jerome Game, in an excellent review of *Antifreeze*, remarks that Sutherland "[succeeds] in avoiding any demonstrative, didactic or programmatic stance. This work is eminently militant, and political, but in a forceful way, artistic rather than literal", this seems to me genuinely important. It is as if Sutherland's work is resolutely pitched against systematisation, always pushing past one dichotomy to then reach and push through another to then reach and push through another, as if hurtling with a gurney through the swing double-doors of a long hospital corridor.

To order *Antifreeze, Quid,* or *100 Days*, visit www.barquepress.com, or write to Keston Sutherland or Andrea Brady, c/o Gonville and Caius, Cambridge, CB2 1TA
To order *The Rictus Flag*, visit http://www.manson88.freeserve.co.uk/op or write to Peter Manson, Flat 3/2, 16 Ancroft St, Glasgow G20 7UH.
Keston Sutherland's essay on "Bathos" can be found at: http://jacketmagazine.com/15/sutherland-bathos.html
Jerome Game's review of *Antifreeze* can be found at: http://jacketmagazine.com/20/game-suth.html

Lamentable Treatment

SARAH MAGUIRE

Guest editor Saadi Simawe,
Modern Poetry in Translation No.19: Iraqi Poetry Today
King's College, London, £9.95, ISBN 095338246X

WITH THE US currently bent on flattening Iraq in pursuit of its burgeoning imperialist ambitions, surely there could be no more appropriate moment to give a voice to the poets of Iraq in English. In his introduction to *Iraqi Poetry Today*, the editor, Saadi Simawe, says he hopes that "translating poetry might contribute to the appreciation of other civilisations and even to peace in the Middle East". It's heartbreaking, therefore, to report that the admirable sentiments expressed by Simawe are completely scuppered by the unrepresentative and largely appallingly translated volume he has edited.

Let's start with the poets Simawe has excluded from *Iraqi Poetry Today*. I appreciate that the great majority of people reading this review won't know much about Iraqi poetry and may well glaze over at the sight of lots of names in Arabic, so suffice it to say that Simawe himself gives a list of *twelve* poets he refers to as "important" who are not represented here. Out of the three Iraqi poets widely acknowledged as the most significant writing today, Sargon Boulus, Hasab al-Shaikh Ja'far, and Saadi Yousef, only the latter makes it into Simawe's selection. This is like producing an anthology called *Irish Poetry Today* including Seamus Heaney (because he's too famous to ignore) but leaving out Michael Longley and Paul Muldoon. Many of these twelve poets have already been translated into English, sometimes very well, so it's not as though their work (including unpublished translations) is unavailable. Indeed, since Simawe edited a special edition of *Arab Studies Quarterly* entitled "Modern Iraqi Literature in English Translation", he must be well aware of these other translations and translators.

Of the forty poets included here who apparently exemplify Iraqi poetry today, one was born in 1890 (the Kurdish poet Sheikh Selman), and five others between 1900-06. Fourteen are dead; some died quite recently, others, such as Badr Shakir al-Sayyab, as long ago as 1964. One, Ronny Someck, also crops up in *MPT No. 14: Palestinian and Israeli Poets*; in that volume he counts as an Israeli poet, having emigrated to Israel from Iraq aged nine in 1960. Whilst any anthology of contemporary poets is bound to create controversy about who's in and who's out, it's worth noting that a large number of the poets found here were *completely* unknown to the leading Arab poets and academics I've contacted. One, Sajidah al-Musawi, a senior female member of Iraq's National Assembly, is even a mystery to the editor; and another, Jawad Yaqoob, died age thirty-six last year before publishing any of his work at all. Why these two poets were included, while twelve poets acknowledged to be "important" were left out, is a mystery. The problem is that many people reading this edition of *Modern Poetry in Translation* will be completely new to Iraqi poetry, and will unwittingly regard it as an honest and definitive selection of contemporary poetry from Iraq. Already the *Guardian* has republished part of Simawe's introduction (though not his list of excluded poets) and selections from some of the poets in the volume.

Serious reservations about Simawe's skewed version of who's who in contemporary Iraqi poetry notwithstanding, what damns this volume beyond redemption is the scandalously low standard of translation. Consider the opening of "The Happiest Man in the World" by Gzar Hantoosh, which, in the hands of Simawe and his co-translator Ellen Doré Watson, has become, "Lushly I walk, like flowers under the bitter orange, / towards my friend the poet". *Lushly I walk*? Has anyone, ever, walked *lushly*? And how is walking lushly "like flowers under the bitter orange"? Poor Hantoosh will hardly be the happiest man in the world if he ever discovers how his poetry's been mistreated in English.

Not all the poems in this anthology are quite so bad. Most of them are merely frustratingly mediocre or pedestrian. Like these lines, picked at random, by Shakir al-Samawi, from a poem called "Wake" (which I presume means "awake" rather than "a wake") from a short sequence called "Quartets of Inner Whispering", translated by Simawe and Chuck Miller:

> Midnight sleepless heart
> no companion or thought to still the loneliness
> no dream to redeem the soul
> the perplexed eye sees complete desolation.

Here, as elsewhere, no effort has been made to turn Samawi's lines into poetry in English.

One of the perversities of *Iraqi Poetry Today* is that some of the poems ruined here are already available in good English versions. For example, two poems by 'Abd al-Wahhab al-Bayyati, "The Birth of Aisha and Her Death" and "Elegy for Aisha" can be found in Salma Khadra Jayyusi's excellent anthology, *Modern Arabic Poetry* (New York; Columbia University Press, 1987: the best available introduction to Arabic poetry if you're interested). In Jayyusi's edition, these poems are beautifully translated by Sargon Boulus (one of the three major poets excluded from *Iraqi Poets Today*) and Christopher Middleton; here, they're rendered as a ham-fisted embarrassment. Ditto Muhammad Mahdi al Jawahiri (at his peak in the 1930s and '40s, so not exactly writing "today"): his "Lullaby for the Hungry" appears in Jayyusi in a lyrical version by Issa Boullata and John Heath-Stubbs, the opening of which begins:

> Sleep, you hungry people, sleep!

The gods of food watch over you.
Sleep, if you are not satiated
By wakefulness, then sleep shall fill you.

The version in *Iraqi Poets Today*, translated by Terri De Young, opens:

1) Sleep, hungry folk, sleep
may the food gods protect you,
2) Sleep, for if you do not eat your fill
awake, then surely you will be in dreamland.

Something especially strange has happened to the Kurdish poets. The great Bekes (Faiq Abdulla Beg) is rendered into English in doggerel, as the opening of "Bright Star" demonstrates:

You bright star of the space
About you I am in a mess
I watch you but cannot guess
Who's set you in that place?

But at least Bekes is represented by poems addressing the heavens. The readers of *Iraqi Poets Today* will go away with the impression that Bekes's son, Sherko Faiq (here inappropriately given the Americanised title of "Bekes Jr"), one of the most admired poets in Kurdish Iraq, can produce nothing but sentimental, simplistic propaganda. The same is true of the other four poets writing in Kurdish, whose poetry as presented here is singularly crude and bloodthirsty.

It's no surprise, perhaps, that the most enjoyable poem in this anthology is absolutely untranslatable: a transcription of a largely-improvised performance by the most popular Arab poet, Muzaffar al-Nawwab, whose cassettes (he doesn't publish his poems) are passed eagerly from hand to hand. The extraordinary skill and complexity of his puns, rhymes, rhythms and references, his ability to joust with the range of classical Arabic poetry, are simply beyond representation in English. What does come across, even in this pedestrian version of a very old poem (recorded in 1977), is the scale of his task, the intensity of his vision, and the scabrous vitality of his attacks on the Arab political establishment.

Only two poets out of the forty here are well translated, by which I mean that the translations read as poems in English might. One is the aforementioned Israeli Ronny Someck, translated from the Hebrew by Vivian Eden. The other is the leading Iraqi poet, Saadi Yousef, who, unusually for an Arab poet, already has a book of (excellent) translations published in the US (*Without an Alphabet, Without a Face: Selected Poems*; Graywolf Press, 2002). Perhaps it would have been a step too far for Simawe to set his translators loose on Saadi Yousef. He's simply too important, and too well translated already by Khaled Mattawa, to be subjected to such treatment. (It's a real pity Simawe didn't also include Mattawa's wonderful translations of Fadhil al-Azzawi, rather than the inadequate versions published here.)

It's the warmth and humanity of Saadi Yousef's inclusive poems which mark him out as one of the great poets writing in any language today. He has revolutionised contemporary poetry in Arabic, through his tender attention to the details of everyday life, and through his rhythms, which are grounded in those of everyday speech. This fragment, from a long poem called "The Trees of Ithaca", presents perfectly his own generous achievement:

He is building boats out of the ribs of speech
unfolding sails out of the scent of lemons
and bringing nearer cities that were ravaged by plagues
and raiders, and brothers, and history…

Sometime around 2230 BC, a Sumerian poet wrote the earliest known lament for a city ravaged by war. The city in question was Nippur, for thousands of years the religious centre of ancient Mesopotamia, the world's first civilisation. Today, Nippur is a great pile of dusty Sumerian rubble in the desert 100 miles south of Baghdad. As I write this on the eve of St Patrick's Day 2003, I wonder how many more laments Iraqi poets will need to write in the years to come.

Standing Still and Walking in Suffolk

ANDREA BRADY

R. F. Langley, *More or Less*
The Many Press, £3.50 inc. p&p, ISBN 097326366

R. F. LANGLEY'S is a slow poetry. It has emerged slowly – his first collection, from Carcanet in 2000 (when the poet was 62), included just seventeen poems. I counted six chapbooks since 1978, the latest – *More or Less*, published by the Many Press – including just seven poems on 18 pages of text. One of these, "No Great Shakes", was published in the 1994 *CCCP 4 Poetry Archive*. In an interview with Robert Walker in *Angel Exhaust* 13, Langley explained that his poems arise from solitude and relaxation – "Which means it doesn't happen very often". The work accrues over "ten years or more" in scattered lines, fragments of possibility whose rereading eventually begins a whole poem.

Such gradual composition produces poetry that can seem, in the Objectivist manner, to dwell in dissociated units, rather than the broad sweep of a total lyric. That is, the development is in the stanza rather than the poem as a whole. But as Peter Riley has argued, "these units are completions: they are not unitary solids, they bear tensions and resolutions within them by contrast, contradiction, shift of tone and mood, sudden exit, resolution at the level of image and so on". For Riley, Langley's poetry is a "sequence of complete poetical actions". As a result, "the epiphanic belief becomes literary and socialised. These are no longer 'his' moments; they can enter a different life because they are not trapped in a circumstance. The craft of their forming, the traditional poetical skills of constantly accurate comparisons, lift them out of the particular in their very fidelity to it, and we take them on as unrecognised instances. It is our job to find them a home".

It is notable that in his observations of churches, fields, houses, and museums, Langley is drawn to the particular contents, to the micro-details of the constituents rather than bigger architectural problems. His poetry rests among the moveable goods, the wineglass, the Songware bowl, the spider, and the butterfly. These are the details which reveal themselves to patience. If, as Riley argues, Langley escapes from "circumstance" into a socialised epiphany, perhaps it is by stopping. Langley recalled one such epiphanic moment: "Oh yes: standing under a tree for an hour-and-a-half. One peculiar evening, that's the biographical centre of it: I walked out of the village at dusk and, as is extremely unusual nowadays, I stood for an hour and a half by a track and no-one came anywhere near me. And it just occurred to me that I ought to stand without moving at all for that length of time and see what happened. Not even turning my head. A lot of rabbits came up and sat on my feet. And moths whipping about within inches of me. A feeling that you might get through to what was really there if you stripped off enough."

Langley tells this story as an example of the autobiographical nature of his poetry. His long discussion of the origins of the poem "The Upshot" in that same interview is revisited in a selection from his journal, dated August 1992 (published in *PN Review* 147), where he recounts a visit to a church in Westhall, Suffolk. He was joined in the church by three determined and inquisitive tourists, whose presence offers an opportunity further to specify his rules of engagement. "Delightful to find people engaged in such investigation, with a mind to it, placing and stating here, where, as they say, it seems so remote you feel you have found it. But the glory is not in these quibbling sorties, however innocent and however much a way of paying tribute to what is. The unspeakable standing of silence, stillness, insistent gentle, combing gold, set in dead white and cooled-out limegreen." Langley idealises a mode of seeing which is attentive to detail without pedantry, investigative without penetration: i.e., not a search for criminal or corrupt design, not a placing of the body (or, by extension, the active self) within the field of what is seen. It is by standing still, becoming immobile, that the quick-eyed human gains access to the secret life of nature.

Surprisingly, he goes on to describe this mode of being as a condition of pure alienation; all flesh may well be grass, but touching grass husks "you have not touched, because their thinginess is so dense, so alien that, though it dents your fingertips, the dent takes the fingertips away from you, into the place beyond". The body disappears, its vivid motions petrified by contact with the ultimately other world of nature. If nature is in constant motion, "the twitchy stems of / grasses make quick snatches in / the air that passes", then the necessity to be completely still might reduce something essential about human life. Langley describes what is reduced as the instrumentality of vision: "things becomes things that you've got to step round or walk over or something. They instantly become part of your map, as it were. Whereas if you stand absolutely still, then they might not be part of any map at all. You 'see' the place when you haven't got any designs on it".

Langley claims Melanie Klein and W. R. Bion among his influences. Reflecting this discussion through Klein's theory of object relations, I'd suggest that for Langley, knowledge of nature is gained when the drive to know the object through relation is halted – when the driven self comes to a standstill. If such drives are fundamental to the formation of the self, then Langley's poetry seeks to overcome the splitting of the person from the object world by repressing the driven self. It is also notable that the poet frequently describes human life and mortality through objects. In "After the Funeral", he writes that "Nothing slabbered about Pauline's death", although a bowl rings when a hand taps its millennial surface in the "Ceramic Gallery" (the Percival David Foundation of Chinese Art in Gordon Square). As an excerpt from Langley's journal (*PN Review* 148) describes, it's through the physical presence of objects that the vacancy left by his friend's death becomes speakable. Eventually, the enduring delicacy of the Chinese ceramics mixes with a kind of blazon to Pauline. "Henan black ware. Oil spot glaze, like droplets of oil floating on water. Like eyes in a photograph floating on the occasion of the party she was asked to as one of the residents."

Paulina in *The Winter's Tale* shows to Leontes the artistic relic that comes to life, in one of literature's great moments of wish fulfilment, a ludicrously literal enactment of the Horatian *locus classicus* about poetry's capacity to outlast dumb brass monuments. In Langley's poetry, it is not the quick but the still who become part of nature; and nature's renewals offer their reassurance alongside a perennial art. "Sixpence a Day" takes as its subject the speaker's own mortality, in celebration of the pure joys of observation:

> There seems
>
> to be no limit to
> the amount of life it
> would be good to have, just
> fingering the thickness
> of a leaf.

But as *More or Less* concludes on the day of Pauline's funeral,

> I forget what is
> left of the leaves. But it's
> a knuckle that keeps rapping
> the bowl, so that it rings.
> So that it rings and rings.

In these simple lines, the residuum of life is forgotten, the "leaves" are left, but so is the fearful meditation on what is "left of" the leaves – their decayed remnants – and the remaining lifetime they represent. That ecstatic flare of repetition in the final line offers a possibility of continuance; the begging bowl and bones played by the clown's dismembered knuckles (his "own / knuckles are the bones he's thrown" in "Experiment with a Hand Lens") are transformed into a writing hand in perpetual, commemorative motion.

The link between his friend's name and Shakespeare's *Winter's Tale* is not a coincidence. Langley has said that Shakespeare is a major influence: "I suppose if there's a single person that's influenced me steadily all the way through, fed me, as it were, day by day, it's Shakespeare . . . that's influenced me more than anything else, I would think: pure Shakespeare: quoting from him, and image themes and basic ideas, yes, he cuts through and underlies the whole lot." In *More or Less*, the poet declares himself "no great Shakes". But the poems are filled with Shakespeare: the title "Cakes and Ale" recalls those festive pleasures which Sir Toby Belch defends against the Puritan kill-joy Malvolio in *Twelfth Night*; elsewhere the bumbling director from *A Midsummer Night's Dream* is addressed: "Peter Quince, it's / not knavery at all!" Lear himself might be hiding in "Still Life with Wineglass", as he who "did choose the third sister" finally, when she became his fool; a Shakespearean clown dangles among the verses too.

Otherwise, the poems include distinctively English characters – "old Harry", Jenny, deaf John, and Langley's well-known familiar, Jack. Jack has already had a few poems all to himself; he appears briefly here in "No Great Shakes", in the form of "Four worn Jacks turn churlish / in the shaking / hand, grinding uneven teeth." Jack inspires the poet by the multiplicity of his kind: "the dozens of columns in the Oxford Dictionary on the word 'Jack'.

And everything you can do with Jack, a sort of commonality of humanity that Jack might represent. And all the different combinations he's been in: the names of flowers, Jacks and Jills, and Jack in the Beanstalks, and jack in the boxes and how Jack turns into Tom and all the rest of it. You know who Jack is don't you? he's that little figure you see running along beside the train jumping over the hedges and swinging from the telegraph poles." A Kleinian might see Jack as a projective identification which enables the ego to be incorporated into nature while remaining in motion. As "The Barber's Beard", a poem published in the *Form Books Occasional Paper,* relates,

> I stop and stand where paths cross on
> a Wednesday afternoon. Where else am I?
> Somewhere there is a story being told.
> I recognise Jack's voice that's quietly
> telling it, as he describes how a man
> is standing underneath a tree. How he
> can see the standing of the man.

This reassuring figure gives Langley an opportunity to describe himself in the epiphanic moment of stillness recounted above. As the image in the mirror whom the speaker shaves, Jack is also a version of the self, always on the verge of slipping away. The poem continues through a series of conditionals – "Suppose . . ." – and concludes with a note on practice:

> Then it would seem that all the answers
> could be ticked. As if the nouns, detected in
> the depths, began to glimmer deeper yet
> beneath the things, so all the secret eggs
> grew wings
> > [. . .] Scuttling verbs
> could trap elusive opportunities
> among unlikely roots.

If the poem's imaginative projections became real, then the poet himself (crucially, along with his readers) would come closer to Adamic language; poetry would find its own place in nature. At that moment, Jack thinks "he might count the flocks" – thus employing the magic of enumeration which, elsewhere, Langley relates through the Sanskrit root "pu" to both "pure" and "compute". "Counting things is the purest way you've got of knowing things. Just to put them into numbers. And it's either adequate or it's not adequate . . . . The search for certainties. That's what it's about. As usual". Pure mathematics is a language whose Platonic potential for description exceeds poetry's naming of the "elusive opportunities". But at this moment the birds fly off, and "Jack and the poet and the pronouns shrug".

Jack is a projection of the poet into nature, a kind of Everyman who possesses the mischievous energies of a Renaissance jape, and a familiar whose common energy radiates through the multiple definitions ascribed to his name. Langley has revealed his loyalty to the etymological dictionaries, a characteristic he shares with J. H. Prynne; and like Prynne, Langley's poetry demonstrates a scrupulous expertise in naming. In *More or Less*, birds, insects, and plants are described with a naturalist's precision: "Soft pappus strings out like a / search party"; "Rabbits are kindling in their burrows"; "Marram shoves its stems through sililca"; "A clink of chitin as eight knees slightly clench". Peter Riley has used Langley as an exemplar of modernist precision which does not give way to obfuscation; in Langley's work, Riley writes, "I don't see any shift into an exclusive metonymic zone. I don't see any revolutionizing anti-writing or espousal of ugliness as method." For Riley, this poetry maintains the "total view of the possibilities of poetical language" characteristic of "unofficial" poets in the '60s and '70s before the "burning of the boats", when "a more denunciatory modernism" arose and "began to read itself as a sectarian option". Several readers comment on the occasional difficulties of criticising Langley's poetry in the absence of the autobiographical detail he has provided for a poem like "The Upshot". At the same time, the seeming lack of ambition of these poems seems to confuse us: if, as Matthew Welton wrote (in *PN Review* 135), "to read this work is not a process of decoding the poems' symbols", then what is it? Is it really an indulgence of "those neat little pleasures of sound rather than some principle by which a poem's structure may be ordered"? Is Langley's expertise a kind of fetishization of the specific in the absence of the kind of macroscopic critique we might expect from Prynne?

Langley himself advocates literalist readings; "I would tend to prefer 'The Red Wheelbarrow' sort of imagery where there isn't that sort of metaphorical foisting. There's just an opening up to what is there in front. With things mattering about it." That things simply "matter" in themselves, by their nature, their life, and their appearance, is not currently a preoccupation of "unofficial" poetry; and Langley's poetry is sufficiently awkward in its syntax and its discursive ambit to keep it out of the main stream. Thus, when his *Collected Poems* was shortlisted for the Whitbread poetry award in 2000, the judges referred to him as "one of poetry's best kept secrets". Langley's dedicated readers might describe his reclusion, from publication or from autobiographical explicitness in his highly personal poems, as a choice – as Iago puts it in Othello – to be "poor as winter" rather than possess "riches fineless", and by such possessing live in constant fear of decline.

I'd like to conclude with that finally laconic villain because Langley constantly confronts his reader with the ethical problem of persuasion. Although Riley says that "his poetical temperament is non-persuasive", not tendentious or critical, it seems to me that Langley's poetry regularly incorporates benign, non-binding persuasion with very interesting results. Thus, the poems in *More or Less*, perhaps more than previous collections, plant many illusory commands in the curls of the ear. They use a dramatic direct address which is both menacing and comforting, guide and misguide. In "Cook Ting" a poem included in *April Eye* (a festschrift for Riley), the voice commands you to "Look about and wipe the knife. / But there's more, there's more. Rubbing it / out will prove there's no nub of the matter". Is this a violent dissection, the knife with a "blade so sharp it can dance round / the joint" a murder weapon, or an episode of professional butchery? If the butcher carving up the carcass is a workmanlike version of the poet, surely this is an unfavourable comparison, not the kind of approach to the subject Langley's benign observation would condone. However, as Burton Watson's translation of the Taoist text by Chuang Tzu (in *The Complete Works of Chang Tzu*) reveals, Cook Ting's craft depends on accurate observation.

Cook Ting laid down his knife and replied, "What I care about is the Way, which goes beyond skill. When I first began cutting up oxen, all I could see was the ox itself. After three years I no longer saw the whole ox. And now I go at it by spirit and don't look with my eyes. Perception and understanding have come to a stop and spirit moves where it wants. I go along with the natural makeup, strike in the big hollows, guide the knife through the big openings, and follow things as they are. So I never touch the smallest ligament or tendon, much less a main joint.

His carving follows the composition of the object itself, and is guided by spirit rather than physical vision. As a consequence, Cook Ting doesn't need to change his knife in nineteen years – any more than the poets Langley and Riley have to change their methods. Cook Ting, an artisan of meat, represents those instances when the poet can flash over his material, his precise vision and knowledge differentiating him from the violent hack.

The imperative direct address in "Cook Ting" is a striking feature of all the poems in *More or Less*. In the opening poem "Cakes and Ale", "you" are Luke Skywalker in "the sequence in the bar / on an outer planet". The monstrous customers threaten to tear you apart, and there's no Obi-Wan Kenobi here to save you; your only hope is an appeal to the "wonderful barmaid, who is / all their mothers still" and who suckles all comers at the handles in "the middle of her rosy, / pumping heart". Like all Langley's work, this poem uses repetition and internal rhyme – but here they are devices which seem calculated to stir up nursery terrors. Half dream, half memory, the poem concludes with the transformation of the bar into a simple pub, the focussing of the barmaid's million hands into "a simple pair".

Thus, even in its most direct and narrative examples, this poetry is about observation, the right and wrong ways of seeing. Notably, this is the only poem which is mostly about other people – and here as in "After the Funeral", people are specified through objects: the specific richness of their elaborate medieval outfits. Several poems reflect on inside and outside, the house with all its contents – as Langley said about an earlier poem "The Ecstasy Inventories", "objects in a way take you close to people, I suppose, and yet they don't as well, of course". As the recorder of those inventories, the poet also gets to look past the house into the natural world. In "Still Life with Wineglass" he gets someone to set up his folding chair by the south door, where he plays the

> ticket collector. Nothing
> comes in but thistledown which
> scarcely touches the floor and
> was never supposed to pay.

But somebody pays. Langley's poetry employs persuasion because the absence of spoken coercion is not the absence of coercion. The invitation to pause and dwell on the particular details and moveable goods which Langley's poetry issues with such generosity, is so sufficient that we might be tempted not to think about the church, the field, the house, or the museum. What then would be a way out of radical alienation, if nature only gives way to us when we are still as stone? As Langley notes in his journal, "The utter loneliness of all things in the extensions of time and space, left and left and altogether left, so that even the fragment of freestone you take with you in the glove compartment, on the dashboard ledge by the steering wheel, means that the journeyings of the car can never take place, since all place is intraversable, still, in the speeding that can't be taking it away. The car stops in the stone. The stone stops in the car."

Langley's poetry seeks a kind of vision which is not instrumental; his beautiful observations, with their constantly sensitive embodiments, open up many important phe-nomenological doubts. But in the end, "The needles are / green. The bird knows it is pink". In opposition even to the explicit precision of this poet's language, the chaffinch's call, "pink pink", is an instance of nature restoring to things their own best names. Whatever the poems may whisper about dilemmas of perception, they often come finally into focus as a misperception clarified and opposed by a true perception. This clarity, given to retirement, is not much with us, in the rush of war.

To buy *More or Less*, write to John Welch at 15 Norcott Road, London, N16 7BJ.

Walls Come Tumbling Down

PETER MANSON

David Kinloch, *Un Tour d'Ecosse*
Carcanet, £6.95, ISBN 1857545168

DAVID KINLOCH'S PREVIOUS collection, *Paris-Forfar* (Polygon 1994), was one of the defining works of recent Scottish poetry (it's certainly my favourite Scottish book of the 1990s). At a time when my own interests centred rather exclusively on the contemporary British and North American avant gardes, Kinloch's work came as a bolt from the blue. Marrying a deep and eclectic awareness of modern European poetry to an affinity for synthetic language which rewrote MacDiarmid as an antiquarian-voluptuary, Kinloch emerged (in that book's amazing centrepiece "Dustie-Fute", a long elegy for a gay man who died of AIDS) writing poetry as extraordinary as any Scot has since the death of W. S. Graham.

If I am less amazed by the book under review, that's partly because *Un Tour d'Ecosse* privileges the more occasional side of Kinloch's writing (beautiful as that can be) over the layered slipperiness of his most language-centred – and, to me, most original – work. Which is to say that I came to *Un Tour d'Ecosse* with the highest expectations, and that if these are not met, nonetheless, this book contains much that is excellent.

Some of the most powerful poetry in *Paris-Forfar* had to do with the awakening of a gay sexuality, and with coming out. The poetry of *Un Tour d'Ecosse*, by contrast, is very much out there to begin with: the gym-shy schoolboy of "Section 28" doesn't need anyone to "promote" homosexuality to him, he already knows he's gay. Autobiographical poems about home-making and idyllic holidays (and the mind-altering "Conversion", where memories of the poet's conversion to Catholicism come back to him during anonymous sex) set a predominantly optimistic tone, only to have this undercut by the remarkable, angry "Wall":

> Look at the wall, the sweet and lovely
> Wall we carry with us in public places.
> Even in meadows when we rest it
> For a second on muscular buttercups,
>
> Its tinyness glimpsed from the distances
> Of outer galaxies is not as small
> As the monstrous little voice
> I use to whisper to you through its chink.

The poem's oddly multivalent ending,

> Smash wall!
> Smash the person of wall
> And the person
> Of pure moonshine!

can be read variously as an exhortation to break down the walls of public decorum, as a gay-basher's revulsion, and as a jag of internalised homophobia. It's one of Kinloch's finest achievements.

Better still, though, is the long prose piece "Des Lits de Guibert (Of Guibert's Beds)", imagining a visit to the Hebridean island of Lewis by Kinloch and the French novelist Hervé Guibert. The skill with which Kinloch differentiates the voice of the grumpy, dying novelist from that of his wide-eyed guide is impressive for a writer who has (to my knowledge) published no fiction, but it's the prose-poetry that remains inimitable:

> *Rossignol! Rossignol!* Each cry bursts a T-cell. Count! Count! Each note is a footstep in my blood, each enemy that comes has a different mask and name. I count the multitudinous names of beds: *lectuli, triclinium, lectisterniacor, lectica* sheepishly somersault beneath my lids. Which one will I die in? Towards dawn, I am the queen-pin in a sickly "lever de la reine" assisted with my regalia by vying buddies. *Rossignol!*

The title sequence is sadly, I think, the weakest part of the book. Written as a poetic dialogue between Walt Whitman and Federico Garcia Lorca, who are engaged in an imaginary cycling-tour of Scotland, it stands or falls on whether or not the reader finds this kind of thing funny or moving:

> Great gorgeous creature of gamboge and black!
> I pin you to my beard, I fasten you
> Upon the snowfield of my whiskers.
> Shrouded bard of another land
> Here is the exquisite flexible door of the sea.
> Let us suffer its changes together.
> ("Camerado")

I've always found Kinloch's humour to be most effective when it's at its angriest, as in the quietly devastating "Three Wee Frees" (from *Paris-Forfar*), a response to bigoted journalism. "Un Tour d'Ecosse", though it makes an eloquent plea for tolerance in post-devolution Scotland, is simply too good-natured a rigmarole to have much bite. Maybe the sequence just has too many echoes for me of the American poet Jack Spicer's much more successful act of ventriloquism in *After Lorca* (1957).

The book contains several translations and adaptations of French poetry (Kinloch is Senior Lecturer in French Studies at the University of Strathclyde), from the unforgettable "Ode tae Borborygmusses (eftir Valery Larbaud)":

> Rift n' pump! Rift n' pump!
> Deep curmurrin uv yer tummy an yer trollie-bags

to this, from "The Year of the Dragon", by Emmanuel Moses:

> You're not so wild about my
> Latest poems, why deny it?

– lines to disarm any critic, and all the more discombobulating for their appearance in a *translation*.

Kinloch sometimes seems a little afraid of his plain style, twisting it into over-easy poeticisms ("I wince, you smile and we / Hopscotch on the dappled / Paving of our easy-ozy inscapes"), and I wish he would stop using nouns as verbs; but his capacity for building larger structures out of individual poems (one of the most memorable aspects of *Paris-Forfar*) is undiminished. The unspoken barrier of "Wall" is placed next to a prose-poem on "The Thresholds of a Scottish Parliament" ("Within the door-stane smeddum of the thresholds of a Scottish Parliament the delicate hyphens pivot, rocking its peoples inwards, outwards to the translated melodies of Carmichael's blessing"), leading on to a heart-breaking evocation of human solitude in "The Barrier", echoed by the comic, loving entanglements of the wakeful and sleeping partners in "Bed".

Such ramifications extend outward from the most straightforward-seeming of these poems, making this a collection whose coherence and pleasurable complexity increase with every reading. It's still not my favourite of Kinloch's books, but it's grown on me by stages and I'd recommend it to anyone.

Open All Hours

WILLIAM CORBETT

Tom Raworth, *Collected Poems*
Carcanet, £16.95, ISBN 1857546245

AFTER FORTY YEARS OF publishing poems far and wide, Tom Raworth finally has a big book of poems from a British publisher. His *Collected* is a doorstop, brick enough to hold open the door between British and American poetry. That Raworth has long been welcomed with open arms in America, and made himself at home there, is evident throughout this book. The three blurbs are by American poets, Robert Creeley, Lyn Hejinian, and Bill Berkson; dedicatees of early poems are Ed Dorn, Ron Padgett, and Kenneth Koch; Raworth's selected poems, *Tottering State*, was published in 1984 by The Figures Press of Berkeley, California; and of the impressive number of books he has published, at least half of them were published by American small and smaller presses. Which is not to say that Raworth is an American poet. He has been embraced there – or, I ought to say, here, since I write this in Boston – because he is as new and fresh in American poetry as he will now be to British poetry at large. If Philip Larkin's half-joking "I'd travel to China if I could return that night to sleep in my own bed" represents Englishness in its most emphatic refusal to look beyond the sceptered isle, then Raworth is an internationalist ready to travel anywhere at a moment's notice. More to the point, if we accept the imagination as a sovereign state, then he carries her passport, which means that he will always leap over boundaries where he finds them. From the start – and it is one of his poetry's most attractive features – Raworth has written poems that are unusually open to the reader's participation. For some, it will take time to adjust to the freedom Raworth allows; and others will recoil from what they may think of as chaos.

Raworth is a poet of nerves and intuition, a highly sensitive instrument capable of registering what Charles Olson once described as, what is "around the bend of the next second". Speed – or, as Bill Berkson has it, "quickness" – is the essential characteristic of Raworth's line. No poet I know reads aloud as fast as Raworth does. In a joint reading he packs his half-hour into fifteen minutes, yet achieves the remarkable by hitting every word just so. You are on a speeding train but you see everything free of whooshh and take it in. Exhilarating, and a little scary. Or perhaps "unsettling" is a better word for the sensation. Raworth takes a little getting used to. With this in mind, he will sometimes, if not often, offer clear statements as to the nature of his work. In an early poem he tells us, "as in the progress of art the aim is finally / to make rules the next generation can break more cleverly". Later, he reminds himself to "tell the dream / not the reason".

It is a consequence of this speed and surge that, while Raworth's poems remember, they do not pause for memory. Images flash in as they do into our consciousness as we walk to work or converse with a friend. It is fair to say that Raworth regards recollection and tranquility as tyrants; he seems to receive poems as if he were a radio the machine poet Jack Spicer imagined all poets to resemble. Although Raworth's poetry is rarely topical, by which I mean addressed to specific events, his poems are always in the now of our increasingly speeded-up moment. As for form: Raworth prefers the lower case, likes naming his poems rather than titling them (I'm assuming names are arbitrary while titles point to meaning), frequently employs collage (he is nimble with scissors and paper and has produced a number of beautiful actual collages), favours writing skinny poems of a word or two to each line, and, over the last decade or so, has based his poems on a six-syllable line. He is less an innovator than a poet who discovered early the means that suited his ends. Over time he has honed these means to a sharp blade that trims and shapes with precision.

One feature of Raworth's work of the past fifteen years or so warranting attention is the almost total absence of proper nouns. His language is simultaneously abstract and concrete, so that the poems take place in a world of their own creation. Quoting at random:

> the faintest pianissimo
> wild clear of pines
> burst into painted flames
> spaciously reveal
> desire of every detail

Because this voice is so assured, the effect is of disembodied authority, almost oracular. But it also, unmistakably, sounds like Tom Raworth.

On the acknowledgements page that lists the many books collected within this volume, Raworth notes that there are no poems from the chapbook *Pleasant Butter* (USA, 1972). The reason for this is that he could not find a copy of the book. This is indicative of Raworth's attitude toward poetry. For forty years he has sent his books out into the world with no thought of a career. He has climbed no ladder; his eye is on no prize. *Pleasant Butter* served its purpose and Raworth moved on. His poems embody the freedom he has pursued, and since he is only sixty-five years old there will be, one hopes, and in his own words, "more forms search telling".

Poetry for Cats and Dogs

JAN MONTEFIORE

Stephen Burt, *Randall Jarrell and his Age*
Columbia University Press, $29.50, ISBN 0321125941

RANDALL JARRELL THE critic needs little introduction to readers of modern poetry, who should be familiar with his brilliant readings of Auden, Moore, Frost, Lowell, and Bishop, and with his devastating poetry reviews. Randall Jarrell the novelist is justly celebrated for the dazzlingly witty, sharply humane *Pictures from an Institution,* one of the very few campus novels to invite the term "classic". But Randall Jarrell the poet, widely known only for his anthology-piece "The Death of the Ball Turret Gunner", is a relatively obscure figure, as he himself complained in "The Obscurity of the Modern Poet": "When I was asked to talk about the Obscurity of the Modern Poet I was delighted, for I have suffered from this obscurity all my life". The characteristically bare idiom of his poems, conversational to the point of prosiness, full of repetitions and hesitations, and seemingly empty of rich metaphors, looks far less attractive than Robert Lowell's flamboyant rhetoric or Elizabeth Bishop's strange, precise clarity.

The achievement of Stephen Burt's excellent book *Randall Jarrell and his Age,* is to show the true subtlety, strangeness, and deep feeling opened up by these apparently unpromising explorations of self and others in the bare style that was Jarrell's trademark, the "plain American that cats and dogs can read" as one poem puts it. Sensitive, learned in twentieth-century poetry, and sophisticatedly attentive to nuance as well as allusion, Burt shows himself a reader of poetry after Jarrell's own heart (and a splendid antidote to the spitefully obtuse recent attacks on this poet by the late Ian Hamilton and Adam Kirsch). He is at home in his subject's *oeuvre* both published and unpublished, in the realm of Jarrell criticism and scholarship (a comparatively small world, true, but far from negligible) where he is generous and just to other commentators, and in the wider contextual worlds of poetry criticism, psychoanalysis, sociology, and philosophy.

More than that, he offers not just an excellent account of Jarrell's poetry but an illuminating and rewarding way to read it. His central argument is that Jarrell's poetry needs to be read as a series of exceptionally subtle monologues in which the speaker explores his- or (more often) herself in relation to a real or fantasied listener, like the little boy in "The Truth" talking to his teacher, or the distraught woman of "Seele im Raum" recalling her imaginary eland (this reading, in which Burt compares the woman's eland to Rilke's unicorn, summoned into being "because they loved it", I found especially illuminating). Conversely, a poem like "The Dead Wingman", where the pilot protagonist circles in dreams the space where his wingman died, which might seem simply to address the man's experience of loss, is also an allegory of the possibilities and limitations of the poetic imagination which cannot redress the mourner's loss but can recognise and acknowledge it.

If all this makes the poet sound like a psychoanalyst, that would be accurate enough. Jarrell's interest in Freud is well known from poems like "Jerome" or "A Hunt in the Black Forest", but Burt goes much farther than this, reading his poems in the light of D. W. Winnicott and Nancy Chodorow to argue convincingly that his poetic explorations of intersubjectivity, love, and death anticipate the insights of object-relations psychoanalysts.

The chapters dealing with psychoanalysis, time, and memory are beautifully done through complex, illuminating, and convincing readings of Jarrell's war poems, his poems about memory and loss, and his own readings of Wordsworth and Proust. Burt emphasises Jarrell's own interest in Wordsworth's poetry, both as a model of "the language really used by men" and because of Wordsworth's interest in children; tantalisingly, he makes a thought-provoking comparison between the little girl in "We Are Seven" who won't accept the fact that her siblings are dead, and the orphaned little boy in "The Truth" who won't accept the lie that his dead father has "gone to Scotland".

The only part of the book that is almost dull is, curiously, the chapter on Jarrell's own prose writing, although – or perhaps because – it is exceedingly well informed. Burt is so concerned first to locate Jarrell's polemical essays about popular culture and TV in the context of mid-twentieth century American critiques of mass culture, and then to show how his critique of mass society anticipates the insights of contemporary thinkers, that he occasionally risks losing sight of his subject's own writings behind his mass of summaries of important thinkers: Charles Altieri, Allen Grossman, John Guillory, Hannah Arendt, Pierre Bourdieu, Emmanuel Levinas, Christopher Bollas, *et al.* dominate this discussion. Consequently, when Jarrell appears criticizing Auden for being seduced by the intellectual lure of Original Sin – "Auden first slipped into this dark realm of Faerie . . . on the furtive excursions of an unbeliever who needs some faked photographs of the Little People for use as illustrations to a new edition of *Peter Pan*, but who ends up as a cook's boy helping the gloomier dwarfs boil toads and snails for the love feast that celebrates the consummation of their mysteries" – the wit and fantasy shine like an authentic deed in a second-hand world. I also find Burt's handling of *Pictures from an Institution* overly thematic; intelligent though his treatment of its Arendtian themes is, one wouldn't guess from his account of the novel at its gaiety and lightness, nor at its perceptiveness about academia (how many teachers could echo Miss Batterson's blandly devastating "There is no book that all of my students have read"?). But this is a very minor flaw, and not an important one, since Jarrell's prose is so immediately attractive that it doesn't *need* an introduction. His poetry does, and Stephen Burt has done the job beautifully.

The Clearing of the Mind

DERYN REES-JONES

Glyn Maxwell, *The Nerve*
Picador, £7.99, ISBN 0330485431

ENTERING THE LANDSCAPE of *The Nerve* we are asked to inhabit a shadowland of hauntings and the haunted, whose presence foregrounds the way in which knowing sometimes resides at the "corner of our lives". The America embraced in *The Nerve*, Glyn Maxwell's sixth volume, is one which includes refugees, beggars, a weatherman predicting hurricanes, women who write letters to men on death row, not to mention a man who holds his own funeral 'to hear the case against him'. This is not an easy habitation, for *The Nerve* is a book suffering in uneasiness, an uneasiness in relation to the word and to the world. Nevertheless, whether through biographical allusion, or dramatisation, or lyric, Maxwell is endlessly curious about the relationship between the mind, and word, and things. In the poem that opens the volume, "The Sea Comes in Like Nothing But the Sea", things become words and are ordered by them as they become the "music of what happens". At the same time, the poem seems to suggest, the experience of their being remains independent of language whilst also impinging on the mind's space:

> . . .a mind, knowing how seldom words
>
> augment, re-orders them before the breaker
> and plays them as it comes. All that should sound
>
> is water reaching into the rough space
> the mind has cleared. The clearing of that mind
>
> is nothing to the sea. . .

But if *The Nerve* is a book about doubt as well as the desire to put faith in language – to find, in Auden's words, a "memorable speech" – it is also a book which suspects that such faith is, by all accounts, an impossibility of the modern world. The tension set up here is between belief and disbelief ("Treasure the nerve / suggesting otherwise; treasure its dis- /belief"), in a life in which there are nevertheless moral choices to be made. And throughout the volume Maxwell circles round ideas of silence and speaking, whether this is the artist who can speak – must speak – or those for whom speaking or not speaking is failure, betrayal, terror. We see this in the child "Genie", for example, who was never able to learn language, because her chance to acquire it came too late; or in the figure of the outspoken Elizabeth Knapp of Groton, accused of witchcraft, who "stuck out her tongue / one sabbath, / and backed the men assembled to all corners":

> The preacher bellowed: 'God has you in chains!'
>
> And in turn the girl replied: 'For all my chains
> I can knock thee on the head if I so please.'
> Which was all she could think of, or her voice
>   Could hold.
> Or the language had. She bit into her hands.

In many ways *The Nerve* is a search for faith. Yet, though desired (and references to a potential divine pepper the book), it seems holiness is also refuted. In "Blindfold" the only kind of redemption offered occurs in a world where language is only itself, the sacred is a trick of the light, and where a parodic Jacob's Ladder is the only available salvation:

> until who comes who's not in on the secret,
> in whose eye there is nothing but *whose eye*,
> one whom the light unwittingly makes sacred,
> who knows no bounds and nothing else, who drops
>   from the white sky
>   rope ladders that start shaking

The journey of the choice between sheep and goats, word and thing set up in the volume's first poem becomes, if not resolved, then ended, in the volume's final poem, "The Snow Village"; perhaps a take on Stevens' "nothing that is not there and the nothing that is", via Frost's "Stopping by Woods on a Snowy Evening":

> In the age of pen and paper,
> When the page was a snow village,
> When days the light was leafing through
> Descended without message,
>
> The nib that struck from heaven
> Was the sight of a cottage window
> Lit by the only certain
> Sign of a life, a candle,
>
> Glimpsed by a stranger walking
> At a loss through the snow village.

Here Maxwell appears to write himself into the knowledge of silence:

> Though the snow erase all traces
> Of his passing through the village,
> Though his step become unknowable
> And the whiteness knowledge.

This volume shows Maxwell off at his finest: technically agile, intellectually questioning, lyrical, compassionate. In *Strong Words* (2000) he wrote that "Poetry is matter that can string itself between the pulse of a life and the silence of a death. The best of it has ends nailed to both: its spaces recall the original and final absence; its marks convey the tremor and burden of the respiring span". The tensions set up in *The Nerve* between the tremor and burden are startling and provoking.

Loss Adjustors

JANE GRIFFITHS

John McAuliffe, *A Better Life*
The Gallery Press, £10, ISBN 1852353279
Dennis O'Driscoll, *Exemplary Damages*
Anvil, £7.95, ISBN 0856463507
Medbh McGuckian, *The Face of the Earth*
The Gallery Press, £10, ISBN 1852353198

EACH OF THESE three very different collections is concerned, in its way, with the exemplary. For John McAuliffe in *A Better Life*, the poem itself is an exemplum. His most favoured form is the short narrative, grounded in everyday detail: traffic jams, cherry blossom, a cot found in the attic of a new home, "bare-chested, cider-drinking teenagers", "an unchipped mug that's emblazoned with 'L.A. Olympics'". Sometimes the poems seem a little too much concerned to generate a conclusion, as when "Moving In" declares ". . . we've cleared away room / For our new table and chairs, for ghosts to roam", and renders the haunting rather too substantial. Elsewhere, however, there is a more allusive open-endedness, as in the riddle "Missing", which moves seamlessly from the substantial to the intangible:

> A yearling in a drained dike,
> A carthorse where the stream changed course,
> A Shetland in a quarry in Kanturk,
> A skull (unknown) beneath the floor
>
> Of the stepdancers' ruined house,
> A goat's head that made the wind sound,
> A king's ransom that was paid twice.
> A rumour taking root underground.

McAuliffe's great strength is to blur the boundaries between what is objective and what is all in the mind. In "A Vision of Rahoon", what at first seems to be an impersonal description of an abandoned housing estate gradually reveals, through the precise accumulation of detail, that it is spoken in the voice of one who has been left behind, who keeps to his room, toasting his friends in home-made wine ("Rhubarb, potato, elderberry"), listening to "The rain frying on the slate roof". The close observation here becomes a parody of that domestic detail which McAuliffe uses elsewhere; the description becomes a form of ritual, the narrator's shoring of fragments against his ruins. Even in poems that are apparently more securely rooted in the everyday, there is a creeping sense of an absence in the local habitations. "A Good Story" moves from the solidity of a remembered home – ". . . square fields, five-bar wooden gates" – through the metaphoric transformation of its surroundings, as "a line of grass" is seen to be "Tall and wild as your tales of the *Titanic* / . . . a good story about / A bottle of smoke", and ends with the realisation that

> . . . you are fragile as paper and your real estate
> A stash of old currency and an expired blue passport
> Inky and true with stamped dates and trade routes.

Allowing the literal and the metaphoric to colour one another throughout the poem, McAuliffe redefines "a good story". The tale and the telling of it are not necessarily distinguishable; the poem shapes what it sees, and becomes less exemplary than lived.

A comparable play between different ways of seeing is in evidence in Dennis O'Driscoll's *Exemplary Damages*. As in his earlier work, O'Driscoll shows a close engagement with the conditions and incidentals of life – with the office workers and clericals, the bloom on the skin of a cherry, the havoc wreaked by illness and old age, the sensuous heat of a summer's day, the meaning of existence. What makes his work interesting is the way in which the greater and the lesser inform one another, so that the incidental is never merely incidental, and the larger questions are brought down to earth. This is nowhere more in evidence than in the title-sequence, which begins:

What are humans for?
To set a pace that ensures
the question will never arise?
To mortify the flesh
in a slum sweat shop

or build up a portfolio
of dot com shares?

O'Driscoll takes a risk here. It is not so much that the question is dangerously large, rather that he seems to provide a choice of small answers, as if the speaker is less distinct than he would like to think from those who fail to ask the question. Given such polarized opposites, it seems the moral will be obvious. However, this fear proves unjustified. In the third stanza the possibility is offered that humans exist in order "To pay lip service to a life / that is always losing face" before going on to suggest that it is the soul which is reflected "in the mirror's / cold sores, sallow skin". O'Driscoll conflates two metaphors so outworn that they are no longer recognised as such, then immediately forces them into a literal context that is itself used as a metaphor. In doing so he suggests not just that there are no easy answers, but that there are no easy questions – an effect that is only enhanced by the run of clichés in the final stanza:

What are we made for?
To live and let live?
To give and take?
To survive the dark night of the soul?
To make more of ourselves?

Where the previous stanzas appear cool, clinical, threatening a satirical assumption that author and reader know better, it here becomes apparent that no such detachment is possible. It is not just that the observer's use of "we" declares himself to be one of the humans under examination, but rather that the questions themselves are weighted by previous usage. The repetition of almost formulaic phrases in a fresh context is connected to O'Driscoll's concern at the loss of a shared religious faith. At the same time, however, it counters such doubts. In "Full Flight", an aeroplane is described as

a speeded-up version

of Bede's fable:
a mechanical sparrow

hightailing it above
that transient banquet hall.

The mechanical sparrow strongly recalls its living counterparts, the sparrows in "Exemplary Damages" whom God used to keep tabs on. Yet even while the qualifying "mechanical" brings the continued existence of that care into doubt, O'Driscoll resurrects the Anglo-Saxon image of the living world as a lighted hall surrounded by darkness, and in doing so himself grants it a beauty, mechanical bird and all. Such tensions are characteristic of the second part of the book, which simultaneously takes pleasure in the sensuousness of the physical world and casts doubt on the truth of appearances. "Tulipomania", for instance, delightedly describes

> . . . the ground-breaking tulip egg
> that incubates in spring, sprouting shoots
> of incandescent plumage: tangerine feathers
> rippled with pink, streaked with aquamarine

and then goes on to enquire:

> Who wouldn't be the better
> for the lesson of those petals,
> dropping off like share values,
> precious metal rates,
> leaving time to meditate on fortune,
> speculate on loss?

If beauty is in the eye of the beholder, O'Driscoll both demands that the eye see clearly and acknowledges the difficulties this entails.

In *The Face of the Earth*, Mebdh McGuckian is equally concerned to change perceptions. Her earth is at once richly itself, seasonal and cyclical, and the locus for myths of origin and metaphor so extensive that it transforms both the subject and the landscape itself. In "Sky Farmer" the sighting of "your fetch in the body-glass / fresh and fresh of the evening" turns into an accumulation of natural detail, wood, and bog "where the plough runs into a globe-corner / over the rise of your hip". In "The Worship of the Plough" the field is at once solid enough to be visited and a metaphor for the speaker to offer herself to a lover. The co-existence of literal and metaphorical reading is a way of emphasising what is cyclical; a way of writing the self into the landscape as in "Mourning Engagement Ring", where the speaker finally merges with the archaeological find:

> I moved like string in a hem,
> the stiff dark clay
> prevailing in my hollows,
>
> sown only on the chance
> of rain with the dead that have become
> the fallen, like stones set in wire:
>
> a boy's anklet, pulverized,
> his wooden bathing shoe, that runs along
> the field lightly reploughed
> and stirring.

Elsewhere, however, what is personal is less easily reconciled with the passage of time. The collection ends with a number of poems for the poet's dying mother, and although her illness too is imaged through the natural world, there is an increased emphasis on a merely human time. In "Hesterna Rosa", "The sundial's shadow falls on nine"; in the final poem, "My mother looks at her watch, / as if to look back over the curve / of her life". She too becomes individual rather than exemplary, and her loss is not fully assimilable:

> the moon's voice
> meets this moon within you,
> brilliant as a forest
>
> around the dusky nightmare
> of the house, where the musicians
> are being forced to play
> death more sweetly.

McGuckian's writing is a talisman against absence, and this collection's faith in renewal is correspondingly hard-won.

While Memory Lasts

STEWART BROWN

E.A. Markham, *A Rough Climate*
Anvil, £8.95, ISBN 085646337X

WHEN I WAS invited, a few years ago, to contribute a piece to a *Festschrift* volume for E. A. Markham, my first reaction was that he was surely too young and active to be the subject of such a valedictory gesture. He is, even now, only in his early sixties, and perhaps more productive than he has ever been – a recent novel, essays, stories, plays, and poems, as well as his full-time commitment as Professor of Creative Writing at Sheffield Hallam. But on the evidence of his new collection of poems, *A Rough Climate*, that sixtieth birthday looming and passing seems indeed to have been the occasion for stock-taking, and for a re-focusing of ambition.

It may not just be the approach of old age though: as the beautifully terrible photograph of volcanic cloud and ash lowering over a green hillside of doomed houses on the front cover of the volume reminds us, Markham grew up in Montserrat, that most unlucky of Caribbean islands. And spiky and controversial as his public attitude to Montserrat may sometimes be, and much as he may in some ways want to distance himself from the exotic othering that is the seemingly inevitable lot of – to use James Berry's phrase – the "West Indian/British" poet, Markham is still very much shaped and focused by that Caribbean childhood. To put it too simply, it gave him his angle on the world. So, sophisticated, ironic, and laconic as he may be in his several personae, learned and worldly-wise as his conversational style suggests (and of course there is no reason why anyone born in Montserrat shouldn't have all of those qualities), one still feels that it's that quirky small-islander take on life and events that distinguishes Markham's writing. Indeed, he more or less says so himself in one of the two fine essays that are included in *A Rough Climate*. So, if Montserrat remains central to his concerns, when the island is by turns flattened by hurricanes and then almost destroyed by the long dormant volcano, it is not surprising that the poet's vision is shadowed by death and the contemplation of "a life skirting comedy".

There are several elegies for lost friends and public figures in this collection; a group of new millennium poems engaging with "the humiliations of this life" as the script of Markham's existence gets both stranger and depressingly familiar; and a batch of poems he groups under the heading "Late (from the last century) News", which are characteristically wry and sceptical takes on the flux and fluster of the cussed lives his several personae endure and, one senses, really rather enjoy. The heart of the book, though, is the group of poems "from Montserrat" which by turns – and often within the same languid poem – celebrates, laments, peoples, and de-populates (and, indeed, investigates the very existence of) that distinctive small place. Markham's island is full of noises. Conflicting and conflating stories are remembered, anticipated, dreamt. Past and present are confused. He is very self-consciously a teller of tales, an urbane dealer in fictions that chronicle "a stressless time and space / free to unbuckle into a life without meaning", although one senses that his real agenda is quite the contrary: to reveal or discover or – more likely – to fabricate some meaning into that life of "tales we used to tell ourselves".

So these are tales of the islands, albeit of Britain and Montserrat (and Australia and Papua New Guinea) rather than of St. Lucia and Trinidad as in Derek Walcott's original. Inevitably, perhaps, that great man of Caribbean letters is very much a presence in this collection – another small island poet with big ambitions mellowing into history – and you sense Markham taking him on, in various ways. In "Hurricane, Volcano, Mass Flight" – a beautifully measured and restrained poem that invokes the safe rituals of domestic rural childhood but is hauntingly about disaster and exile, you sense the example of a poem like Walcott's "Sunday Lemons". He is invoked more directly in what is perhaps the pivotal poem of the book, "Nearing Sixty", which recalls Walcott's "Nearing Forty" as "managing, in the end without bitterness / or pity to rhyme sleep with weep".

Markham's poem, like his life, is less conventional, too chaotic even in the edited narratives of memory for the neatness of regular rhyme:

> For I, too, may have planted a brick
> here or there and watched it grow, like unearned
>   income, into villa,
> casual as the thought of travelling to Australia

Always wanting the possibilities of another life, he is as interested in what might have been as in what has been, and so the poem ends with his discovery of an old spinster lady, life-locked on the island, who had – in their youth – turned down the poet's father's proposal of marriage. Here Markham proclaims her his second mother, imagining – embroidering – the person he might have been, the life she might have led.

Framed by the two autobiographical essays that help contextualise the life these poems contemplate, A Rough Climate is perhaps Markham's most accessible collection to date. Maybe it wasn't too soon for that Festschrift; there's certainly plenty here to celebrate.

We Are Not Worthy

ANDREW DUNCAN

Edwin Morgan, *Cathures: New Poems 1997–2001*
Carcanet, £6.95, ISBN 1857546172

CATHURES, THREE SYLLABLES, is an old name for Glasgow, which appears in the *Life of St Kentigern* (a British figure whose name might remind us of Vortigern), after whom Glasgow's Cathedral is named. Pelagius foresees that "Cathurian towers will ring this hill" (the towers in question are probably the nineteenth-century ones which, inspired by a wish among the city's inhabitants to excel, and encouraged by the site – a range of low rolling hills – now produce a pleasing effect when you look up at towers from the dips). The word may be stressed on the first syllable, like a group of dactylic words presumably from the same language: Lanercost, Lailoken, Lothian, Kentigern, Arthuret.

Many of the poems here derive from Morgan's appointment as poet laureate of Glasgow, and are about local legends or news stories. One subject is Pelagius, a Romano-British heretic whose Latin name has been interpreted as a version of a Celtic original like *Moriganus* or Morgan. The results can sometimes be disappointing: the tale of Madeleine Smith – a strange Romantic death involving cocoa, arsenic, and a Frenchman with a glossy complexion – is thin because Morgan really has no interest in tragedy, the besotted, or besetting ideas. The poem bears no comparison with Sacheverell Sitwell's handling of the same material in *Splendours and Miseries*. But the poem on "John Tennant", of Tennant's Stalk, a tower-chimney, more than makes up. Likewise "Gifts":

> The whistle said: Gather the drum-rolls, roll up the riffs,
> hatful of hooters, splice the sirens with gulls and
> saxes, make a parcel, pack in parker parry parsifal,
> get a blast at last, pass the hat. And hang up that heat
> of the hoot, on the hook. Park your partings. Play in
> array. Sets for all clay.

This poem is a tribute to Roy Fisher, in a strange metrical pattern of staccato parallelism, rippling phrases slipping past each other without adding up to a line.

The poems in *Cathures* are unconcerned with character steeled by adversity, moral principles, the exposition of law, or slow-moving structures. Here is an indicative moment:

> *Drifters* was shown to the Herring Board:
> Even the herring were bored. Sorry John!
> See worthiness? That is Scotland's shame.
> One thing you can say about Glasgow,
> It is not worthy. And neither am I.

This refers to John Grierson's 1928 film on the herring fisheries, and to a Scottish preoccupation with sea fishing. Stephen Tallents was aware that the Secretary to the Treasury had written a book about herring. So the Treasury funded a film directly – the only time they've ever done this. And thus the British Documentary Movement was born.

David Thomson says "Grierson was a harsh, restrictive enthusiast. Although he proclaimed a yearning to liberate and extend film-making, he evolved a narrow doctrine hostile to many other types of cinema, essentially bigoted and unintelligent and isolated by history." *Drifters*, according to *A Biographical Dictionary of the Cinema*, "is symptomatic of the academic, Russian-influenced beauty of much British documentary". Poetry had a certain romance with documentary which also involved a documentary of the self. MacDiarmid, Joseph Macleod, W. S. Graham, George Campbell Hay, and George Mackay Brown all wrote poems about sea-fishing. Morgan, by contrast, isn't interested in what is characteristic or heroic. His towering excellence lies in having a brain fast and alert enough to capture dozens of simultaneous, transient, and puzzling events to which we do not have acquired responses.

The *nouvelle vague* directors reacted against scripts and old-hand actors in favour of spontaneous story-telling. The Scottish *nouvelle vague* didn't make any films. (A movement calling itself the *new swaw* published a manifesto in Peebles in 1963, drafted by John Leuchars Goddard, Aggie Vardabrae, and Frankie Thruffauld, launching a magazine called *Liars du cinema*.) Film-makers didn't go out into the streets of Glasgow with no script and no set, seizing on whatever caught their eye, and relying on performers with naturally expressive movements. Scottish *nouvelle vague* cinema is . . . Edwin Morgan. Morgan is the sensitive mind as contact-sheet, catching undesigned and evolving scenes, cutting from action to action. This is still documentary – but documentary hungry for the transient instead of the durable. The impromptu style contains the possibility of getting primary sensations before the post-processing which adds meaning. When we're surprised, we're all the same. When we're looking at the same thing, we are close to each other.

Scotland is autonomous because its people have always remembered that they were Scottish; but reference to the society of 1707, or 1603, gives no hint of how a free Scotland should dispose of its time. In fact the domain of freedom seems excellently to include small-scale, spontaneous, unscripted impulses, caught before systematisation. The sound poem, in its guise as an autonomous generatable world, seems now to be a rehearsal for a free Scotland.

There a series of twenty poems in *Cathures* called "Demon", about an unnamed devil of provocation whose task seems to be simultaneously to face a poet with reality and to force him to immerse in it, before aestheticising its disorder and damage. His rattling has

> Pungenced, punched, punctuated the
> singing.
> And made the singer devilish angry,
> Devilish fearful, and at last devilish strong.

Know Your Plaice

SIMON JENNER

David Kennedy, *The President of Earth: New and Selected Poems*
Salt, £8.95, ISBN 1876857102
Michael Hulse, *Empires and Holy Lands: Poems 1976–2000*
Salt, £8.95, ISBN 1876857463
John Matthias, *Working Progress, Working Title*
Salt, £8.95, ISBN 1876857412

AS OTHER POETRY publishers dry up, Salt Folio looses a positive deluge of titles from its new Cambridge base. Forty per year are promised, on a print on demand basis. Advertising lies in reviews like this. The volumes are now more handsome too. Probably, in its technical practices, Salt is the way of the future for poetry publishing. The real question, of course, is whether the poems will last.

David Kennedy was co-editor of *The New Poetry*. *The President of Earth* shows him to be a more complex writer than that role would suggest. Even so he retains a certain simplicity. "The Story of Peaches", lyrical and lapidary, recalls his father's sharing a peach tin in a trench at Alamein: "to the last clinging tears of syrup. / I hope I can leave something similar // maybe just passing this one / will be good enough." Refusing to squeeze the last syrup, Kennedy offers an unblinking poetics free of specious closure. Witness, after much development, the end of "Semper Eadem":

> I do things now whether I want to or not
> instead of being fooled by time
> into thinking there's always tomorrow.

Such bleak resolve is characteristic. Also characteristic, however, is an aleatory dream narrative, an associative richness. One instance of this is "The Art of Poetry", in which Kennedy, showing his "New York" credentials, cuts up an interview. Another instance, from the second section of the book, is "Cities": a whirligig of broken sestinas, where last lines become first ones of the next but three poem. Kennedy has to make such containing lines ring, tease out a whacky invention. He does; dream poems like "A Glass Staircase" spin Kennedy's sleeping erudition out to us: "In fact, your life comes through to you in morse / and all too rarely from that shadowy Europe . . ." Other opening lines congregate around this theme: "I can think of better ways to open the caravan / of dreams . . ." ("Soda with Persephone") or "It would never happen in a more dolphin-like civilisation . . . which should tell us / something of how strange we are to ourselves". The openings draw one in, but Kennedy's neatly shifting closures signal, like his evasive subject-matter, a kind of Ashbery rope trick. The journey, as in Cavafy's "Ithika" is all. One arrives at the end of his poems uncertain, but entranced.

Michael Hulse, one of Kennedy's *New Poetry* co-editors, is longer known: *Empires and Holy Lands* is a selected poems spanning 1976-2000. Though more traditional, for the most part, his parodic snatching of other rhymes can be precarious fun. "A Treatise on the Astrolabe", for instance (with its reference not to Chaucer but to Lewis Carroll) hints a riotous subconscious bordering paedophilia: "The slithy toves / are buggering the borogroves . . . They bang and bander at the snatch . . . Maud . . . lies back". Dracula dies of AIDS: "*Fuck Bram / Bram sucks. I suck. Therefore I am . . .*" The prize-winning early "Dole Queue" empathises energetically, though the residual wisdom: "Why . . . are we landed with / a life before death" is more epigrammatic than organic, while "The Essential Auden" (filching Cope) is more schoolboyish than Auden ever was. Hulse's true strength is to be found in other engagements with the past, and in "Five Poems after Winslow Homer" he is at his most shivery, as belles

> pursuing their quest of first causes, stop
> before oblivion's pavilion
> to review from the top
> the proven conclusions of sun –
>
> each one of them a fresh hypothesis
> of flesh . . .

John Matthias's *Working Progress, Working Title* puns as it means to go on, embracing two experimental poems, "Automystifstical Plaice", and the autobiographical "Pages: From a Book of Years". "Plaice" exults in the collaboration between avant-garde composer George Antheil and siren Hedy Lamarr: the result of which is a radio-controlled torpedo. Computer rhymes and mis-readings erupt as lyric interludes. Parisian avant-gardes and the protagonists' films, *Ballet mecanique* and *L'Inhumaine*, allow a *Maximus*-like elaboration of place, or is it plaice? "Antheil"/"Anteuil", and other such dislocations, furnish all the fun: "The Novia poured out the oil the gears were engaged / the études composed and the light bulb / was Americaine. Voila Picabia . . ." But Matthias squashes Antheil's puckishness. He is so *scherzo* a poet that an IT matrix no doubt inevitably suggested itself as means of netting his poetics. But the rigid format confines his wit, which can get lost behind procedural density. Distilled, though, Matthias could be rather wonderful.

Out of the Vortex

JAMES KEERY

David Jones, *Wedding Poems*, edited by Thomas Dilworth
Enitharmon, £12.00, ISBN 1900564874

HOW WOULD YOU review a fifth quartet, if by chance it had remained unpublished for sixty years? The poems published for the first time in this extraordinary monograph take their places immediately amongst the best of the war years; and relocate their author on the map of English poetry. This is a little more than a figure of speech, for Jones really has appeared hard to place.

In *A Map of Modern English Verse* (1969), John Press omits him from the chapter on the First World War because *In Parenthesis* (1937) was "written some years after the Armistice" – then forgets all about him! There is no such place as *The Anathemata* (1952) – "probably", Auden reckoned, "the finest long poem written in English this century". In the classic study by A. T. Tolley, *The Poetry of the Forties* (1985), Jones is listed amongst the contributors to Wales, but is otherwise non-existent. In *English Poetry Since 1940* (1993), Neil Corcoran explores his interrelations with Eliot and Joyce, and with Heaney and Prynne, but closes his fine chapter on Jones and Bunting with "a lesson preached by Salman Rushdie": "English, no longer an English language, now grows from many roots". For all his preoccupation with Roman Palestine, Celtic Wales, Mametz Wood, and Gretchen Trench, Jones's English *is* "an English language", never out of earshot of "Stratford-atte-Bowe" ("Pronounce all French place names as in English", *IP*). *Wedding Poems* locates this poet in *London*, during the Blitz, once and for all.

The two poems, "Prothalamion" and "Epithalamion" were written in September 1940 for the marriage of Jones's friends, Harman Grisewood and Margaret Bailey. Jones borrows Spenser's euphonious titles but also alludes, with Eliotic irony, to the "Sweet Thames" invoked in his refrain. As London was laid waste by the Luftwaffe, Jones lay listening to the "low whine & dull thud away in the distance", inevitably reminded of his "first shell in Xmas 1915":

> Out of the vortex, rifling the air it came . . . the **howling** crescendo's up-piling snapt ... the pent-up violence released a consummation of all burstings out; all sudden up-rendings and rivings-through . . . all barrier-breaking – all **unmaking**.

In Parenthesis: the stunning first incursion of violence into an ironic narrative of yawning, grumbling Tommies and gallows humour – " '01 Ball, is it – there was a man in Bethesda late for the last bloody judgement". "Prothalamion" recalls the "moment" of the Apocalyptic "unmaking":

> At the time of the **howling,** in the days
> of the final desolations, at the precise moment
> of the eclipse:
> Margaret (gentle as falcon, or
> hawk of the tower) with
> Harman, my sweet friend

spread in a vault their bed of unity, to mock

the **unmaking**.

It is a genuinely strange effect – the words echo like the hollow of "a vault" in "an atmosphere of Juliet's tomb", like the ballads of doomed young lords. The "wedding chamber" (*thalamos*) is an air-raid shelter; and the poet cannot in conscience allow happiness the last word:

So have I heard bird-song, beneath the

trajectory zone, at Passchendaele, or seen

flowers lean toward each other, under the sun

that shined to delineate the hate and mutilation

of the Forward Area.

The notes to *In Parenthesis* associate "the Forward Zone" with Arthurian legend, but here the line itself suffers amputation. The fertility of marriage is threatened by "the unmaking", a monstrous, anti-creative "Pernitric begetting" (*IP*). Hope is undermined by dispassionate irony ("zone" can mean a girdle; and "Epithalamion" begins with "Helen . . . and/ the girdle-loosers"), and by an echo of *Ecclesiastes* ("no new thing under the sun", *IP*). Dilworth, who has edited this edition of *Wedding Poems*, notes the Greek for "Apocalypse" in "the time of the ultimate uncovering", but not the direct allusion in "horrors/ unnamed from the foundation of the world" (*Revelation* 13:8). He detects, and admires, a "modulation . . . to loving unity" in "Prothalamion", as contrasted with "Epithalamion": "Margaret cannot really compensate for the calamity of war. The poem refuses". Finely said; but I think both poems refuse.

Their mood is in stark contrast to that of a third new poem, presented in an appendix. "The Brenner, March 18, 1940" is a prayer for peace, inspired by a meeting, during the phoney war, between Hitler and Mussolini – dressed up as the Germanic chieftain, Hermann (Arminius), and the Roman general, Varus, before the slaughter of three full legions in the Teutoburg Forest in 9AD. Jones sends it to Grisewood as a "joke" – a pun on his name, (H)Arminius of Grise(dale) Forest? – but, as he reports, the occasion "thrills me more than I can say". The poem implores Divine Mercy "to see to it that the Out-Isles behave with circumspection". Dilworth admits that "the ennobling epithets" became "politically … inappropriate", but vindicates the "underlying vision".

Dilworth is working on a biography of Jones, due around 2006. I want to read it *now*, but in the meantime, it's clear that he has distilled much of his insight and research into the seventy brilliant pages of biographical and scholarly material – including annotations to Jones's annotations! – that accompany the ten pages of new poetry.

What Will Survive

STEPHEN BURT

Daniel Huws, *The Quarry*
Faber, £7.99, ISBN 0571197116

ECCLESIASTES TO THE contrary, the race for recognition in poetry does, more often than not, go to the swift: well-known poets in Britain as in America bring new books out every three to five years, and longer intervals risk critical neglect for all but the most established. It's no wonder, then, that Daniel Huws has achieved what fame he possesses, not as a poet, but as an authority on medieval Welsh manuscripts: now past his seventieth birthday, the longtime librarian (at the National Library of Wales) has published just two, fairly short, books of poems, *Noth* (1972) and the present volume. Since it contains both *Noth* and an accomplished sestina from forty years ago, *The Quarry* now serves as Huws's collected poems; it will endure when much thicker collections are dust.

Because he works in short, dense forms, dependent on implication and gravity, Huws communicates his powers only when his poems are quoted whole. Here is the title poem, an introduction, not to everything he can do, but to all his poems about memory, childhood, and Wales:

> The quietness,
> They have all scattered
> Into the maze of gorse
> And slabs of rock,
> In tattered jerseys
> And faded frocks.
>
> Ages ago,
> And I still stand
> Caught in the long afternoon
> In the old quarry,
> Face to the wall,
> Counting to twenty.

Not a word of needless description, no explanation, no showing off: just a punning title and two sentences (both of them grammatically incomplete) to sum up youth, sport, nostalgia, pursuit, happiness, and the distance age holds from them all.

The *Noth* poems often look at place and nation: "We know our crags, our climbs, our controlled terrors / As we know our own hearthsides. We manage nicely". Huws now excels at other sorts of description too: one desolate ten-line poem sketches "a kind of Sahara" where "The sun lifts into the sky again / To a chorus of bread and water". As in many of his poems, "Time wavers, / Time falls away", and bare juxtapositions convey the wisdom a worse poet might try to spell out. Huws can create such juxtapositions by compressing time within a few lines, or through close focus on one space, as in "Palais d'Amour":

The cabaret comes to climax
At the lit end of a crowded hall
As a mumbling transvestite thrusts
A cup in the air in triumph.

In shadow beside a disturbed
Ocean of heads a watchful madame
In her own space, to her own music,
Dances her baby to sleep.

Such poetry withstands as much pressure as any reader could bring to any word ("lit", for example, or "own", or "ocean"): it deserves to be memorized. So does the knowingly Larkinesque "First Night":

Open-eyed in bed,
Effigies on a tomb.
Outside is starry and bright-rimmed
Clouds are traversing the window
Making their quick condolence.

Deep in a new first night,
Past all but holding hands,
Not a word, not a stir, nor now
Any sobs any more.

The couple described could literally be sculptures (like those in Larkin's Arundel tomb). And yet they sound to me more like a living couple, awake in bed on the first night after losing a child: such grief, such supple syntax, and such riddles dominate several equally well-made poems.

All of which might give the impression that Huws is unvaryingly serious. He is not: his poems based on songs and nursery rhymes welcome, if not comedy, certainly pleasure:

We found the table bare
And bare the larder shelves.
We slipped to an upper room
And helped ourselves to ourselves.

Even so, Huws certainly stands out most for his most serious short poems, poems about time and irrevocable loss, and about the loyalty to children and childhood (his own and others') which sometimes looks like the poet's chief reason to live. He is happiest when he uncovers evidence that such loyalties are not his alone, as in "The Guardians", whose halting lines suggest that it took the poet a long time to understand what he had seen:

Lift your eyes to heaven
And you suddenly see them,
Two guardian angels,
High above the valley,

Moving apart,
Moving together,
Looping
On invisible swell.

It isn't a love dance,
It isn't a duel.
They are feeding their young.

Huws' manner and matter – and his scholarly career – suggest that he has learned much from poetry in Welsh, and perhaps in other Celtic tongues. Equally, though, he has clear parallels among English-language poets; for instance Edward Thomas, R. S. Thomas, and the American poet Stanley Kunitz. Either Thomas might have encountered the gamekeeper's wife in "Woodsmoke", who laughs as she tells the poet and his companion, "You're the first to have called all winter."

Most favourite new books of poems encourage readers to ask how long they will survive the current fashion; Huws's work raises no such qualms. These small, dense, gravely-spoken poems seek only what Elizabeth Bishop called "the little that we get for free", and try hard to believe that it might be enough.

Thomas, Thomas & Thomas

TONY CURTIS

R.S. Thomas, *Residues*
Bloodaxe Books, £7.95, ISBN 1852245964
The Collected Poems of Roland Mathias, **edited by Sam Adams**
University of Wales Press, £30, ISBN 070831760X
Sheenagh Pugh, *The Beautiful Lie*
Seren, £6.95, ISBN 1854113119
Sarah Corbett, *The Witch Bag*
Seren, £6.95, ISBN 1854113224
Paul Henry*, The Slipped Leash*
Seren, £6.95, ISBN 1854113232
John Davies, *North by South: New and Selected Poems*
Seren, £8.95, ISBN 1854113259
Elin ap Hywel & Graham Davies, *Ffiniau/Borders*
Gomer, £7.95, ISBN 184323078X

TWENTIETH-CENTURY POETRY in Wales was dominated by the three Thomases: Edward, Dylan, and R.S. For much of the second half of the century the pyrotechnics of Dylan Thomas, on the page and in the surviving recordings, were a huge influence: a generation of poets from Wales either aimed for that crumbling grandeur and fell short, or claimed legitimacy in his shadow for their excesses in life and on the page. For instance, Dannie Abse, the most consistently rewarding poet of the second half of the century, whose *New & Collected Poems* has just been published: Cardiffian, Jew, doctor, poet, Londoner, novelist, playwright, Welshman, he has, so to speak, worn with distinction the "white coat and the purple cloak". Abse's first collection, *After Every Green Thing*, accepted when he was a medical student at Westminster but delayed by the post-war shortages and published in 1948, is obviously indebted to and imitative of Dylan Thomas. But Abse was also one of the founders of the "Maverick" group of poets, and his contemporaries, John Ormond, John Tripp, Glyn Jones, and Leslie Norris took Edward Thomas, that most lyrical and elegiac of the Edwardian poets, and also Philip Larkin, with his urban disquiet, as exemplars: they provided ways of not being Dylan Thomas.

The third Thomas – R. S. – whose posthumous poems have been edited by M. Wyn Thomas, is one of the major Christian poets of the past century. *Residues* is a selection of those manuscripts and uncollected poems deemed by Wyn Thomas to be "(by my standards if not by those of R. S. Thomas) of publishable quality". Thomas was one of the most prolific of poets, but it is, nevertheless, good to have the chance to see these leavings. Some are, of course, slight or unfinished, and some have variant versions which allow for rare insights into his art, very few of Thomas's manuscripts having been preserved. Spare and sharp, glinting like diamonds both rough and polished, Thomas's poems illuminate human dilemmas. They are often the records of his sea-gazing, hill-walking, bird-watching, solitary expeditions into the rugged beauty of Wales to find God. More often than not, what the poet-priest finds in that landscape is not an answer or a revelation, but another set of questions, a confirmation of the need to quest. Here is a typical short poem from the new selection, "Festival", in its entirety:

> This Christmas before
> an altar of gold
> the holly will remind
> us how love bleeds,
>
> the mistletoe remind
> how pale and puny
> the knuckles of the few
> fingers clenched upon faith.

It could be the core of a sermon from which tenets of the faith are developed; but it remains, properly, stark and undeveloped. Too often R. S. Thomas's poems are heavy-handed in their metaphors, too arbitrary in their line-endings, but his best work has a startling and visionary power:

> …Circularity
> is endless, yet
> one prayer, slipping
> the reason, speeds out
>
> into the cornerless
> universe so close to God
> as to open a crater
> in his composure.
>
> ("Launching a Prayer")

That final image is profoundly unsettling; it is as if we have to explode our prayers in the face of a cosmic god, firing them off into the never-ending darkness that surrounds our earthly life.

Like R. S. Thomas, Roland Mathias, whose *Collected Poems* have been edited by Sam Adams, had a profound effect on Welsh literature in the past century; though in Mathias' case, it has been as a critic and editor more than as a poet and activist. Mathias was the founding editor of *Dock Leaves* in 1949. In 1957 this became *The Anglo-Welsh Review*, the most significant literary journal in Wales, and then eventually *The New Welsh Review*. The *Collected Poems* is a weighty book with nearly seventy pages of notes and a fifty page Introduction by Sam Adams, himself a poet and former editor of *Poetry Wales*. It is a labour of love and admiration, with the length and erudition of the editorial context indicating that this is a poet of significance with whom the reader may well need assistance.

A writer of fiction and historical papers, Mathias writes poems which are powered as much by his reading of history as by personal experience. He sees himself as rooted in the heritage of South Wales, and seeks to excavate collective memories from the region. His ear knows the Welsh discipline of *cynghanedd*, with its internal rhymes and alliterations, though it is probable that he absorbed this through Gerard Manley Hopkins, that honorary Welshman. He certainly absorbed the power and the risk-taking of his contemporary Dylan Thomas. At his best, Mathias evokes a particular place and a particular way of voicing identity in the way at which the Welsh and Irish have excelled:

> June, but the morning's cold, the wind
> Bluffing occasional rain. I am clear
> What brings me here across the stone
> Spit to the island, but not what I shall find
> When the dried fribbles of seaweed
> Are passed, the black worked into the sandgrains
> By the tide's mouthing. I can call nothing my own.

("Porth Cwyfan")

Mathias's successor as the editor of *The Anglo-Welsh Review* was Gillian Clarke. Hers is the most notable woman's voice in twentieth-century Welsh poetry and she continues to be the outstanding poet working in Wales today; as such, and owing to her intelligent voicing of women's experience, she has provided a clear model for successive generations of women poets in Wales – that of Gwyneth Lewis, Hilary Llewelyn Jones, Menna Elfyn, and, in ways both negative and positive, that of Sheenagh Pugh, Sarah Corbett, and Anna Wigley.

Pugh is a skilled shaper of poems and projector of others' voices. *The Beautiful Lie*, her ninth collection, again shows her control over the dramatic monologue with a sequence in the character of Lady Franklin, the wife of the nineteenth-century explorer. She also includes a sequence of poems based on one of her odder enthusiasms, fan-fiction. Sheenagh Pugh is a poet of the urban and of the media phenomenon, as well as a translator of period European languages, especially German and Russian. She combines erudition and a passionate knowledge of trash culture in a constantly surprising, usually compelling way and would not wish to be referencing in any way the work of Gillian Clarke. The title poem is the key to her aesthetic: the moment we learn to fictionalise, to compose, to lie, we are liberated from the banal:

> When he said "No", I swear it was as moving
> as the first time a baby's fist clenches
> on a finger, as momentous as the first
> taste of fruit. I could feel his eyes looking
> through a new window, at a world whose form
> and colour weren't fixed
>
> but fluid, that poured like a snake, trembled
> around the edges like northern lights, shape-shifted
> at the spell of a voice. I could sense him filling
> like a glass, hear the unreal sea in his ears.
> This is how to make songs, create men, paint pictures
> Tell a story.

("The Beautiful Lie")

Sarah Corbett's second collection, *The Witch Bag*, has just been published. Her world is one of emotions breaking through the surface of everyday life like wounds. Everything, it seems, is portent: food, sex, birth, death – this poet's cycle of experiences are sensuous and heightened in colour, texture and taste:

> I watch you deliver the first,
> A big, black-legged boy you pull
> By the hoof and nose, stretching the ewe,
> Her giving sex opening in one last flood
> Of relief and fluid. We rub the warm
> Back into the lamb, the breath
> In our mouths metal with womb-blood.

("Fold")

The writing is muscular, and textured, and sexual. Where Pugh is a cool, if emotionally engaged, observer, Corbett, whose work does resemble Clarke's, seems always a pained participant. This is especially effective in the sonnet sequence "The Kitchen God", a convincing evocation of food and sex:

> . . . Do you remember
> When I was pregnant? I loved that red spiced
> Soup with lentils, a glob of yoghurt stirred
> In your unleavened bread, salt and pepper
> Tarting the dough, dipped and sucked. So, so nice.

Paul Henry's settings are likewise domestic. *The Slipped Leash* is his fourth collection of poetry and confirms him as an engaging poet of the personal life and the lyrical moment.

Many of the poems are set in the context of the urban and domestic, but all the strongest launch successfully out into realms of wider significance, the surreal even. The title poem observes an old dog's leash which is now used to suspend a nut cage for the birds visiting the garden. The evocation of the "whiffs of him / for all the wind and rain – / sea dog, country dog" fires memories and pushes the poet into introspection: "What misfits we'd have made, / haunting this town's streets, / our walks cut into neat / desperate portions of breath".

Occasionally, he strains the poem and our credulity a touch too far, as in "A Window on the Sea" and "Loving the Beekeeper", which never quite settle their comic purpose; but when he fixes a memory in a short poem such as "Llangors", the effect is clear and poignant. Two young lovers are in an ice-gripped boat which "would have done for a bed / but, older than our years, / we knew, or thought we did, / that the moon on the lake was enough". Has Henry read Michael Longley, I wonder? The Longley of *The Weather in Japan* and *Gorse Fires*? A fine poem such as "Boys" would seem to be pointing that way. Henry is a poet of lyrical discovery.

John Davies is closer to the mainstream of twentieth-century Anglo-Welsh poetry and is much concerned with locating himself and Wales in the wider world. A south Walian long settled in the north, Davies is, with Duncan Bush, Robert Minhinnick, and Nigel Jenkins, a poet much travelled in the USA and its poetry, and his work reflects those experiences. He is equally interesting when he deals with the matter of Wales. R. S. Thomas is, of course, a challenging reference point:

> We stood accused
> of reading him. Wrong
> language, place, wrong century.
> Though his shadows from the fields
> match ours, he made his own world,
> lashed it for not surviving.
>
> ("R.S. Thomas")

In "The Old Language" Davies confronts the anglicised retirement strip that the north Wales coast has become:

> Echoes outlast sound. Listen, nudged awake,
> They too murmur. Says earth's vocabulary
> Of names on scribbled surfaces, it takes
> More than the one tongue to speak a country.

"The Old Language" is from the sequence "Reading the Country". John Davies's body of work contributes to that task. What does it mean to live in this small, beautiful country? What sort of a person, what sort of a writer might that make you?

The two factors other than gender which determine anyone's identity in Wales are their place of birth and their use of the Welsh language. Roland Mathias's poetry is a life-long attempt to locate himself in his history and heritage, necessarily outside of the language. R. S. Thomas was a passionate, aggressive nationalist who preferred to speak (and write prose) in Welsh, but who declared that he could not write his poetry in that language.

Gillian Clarke, Peter Finch, and Christopher Meredith are among those who have learned the language and argue strongly for its use. Menna Elfyn has led the way in publishing poems in parallel text with Bloodaxe, and Gwyneth Lewis is an equally significant poet in both languages. Yet Twm Morys, the poet-songwriter son of Jan Morris, writes in the Spring issue of *Poetry Wales* that his strict metre poems would be butchered in translation and that "I write in Welsh because I'm speaking with Welsh-speaking people. If others would like to join in, well they can bloody well learn the language!" It is a continuing dilemma: does a minority language protect itself by sealing its literature, or is it best served by offering access to non-speakers? *Ffiniau/Borders* by Elin ap Hywel and Grahame Davies brings together two notable poets working in Welsh. These writers, through the project that became this book, "came to understand anew that the poem's energy, either in the original language or in translation, lies in the hearing – and in the willingness of other people to listen". When Elin ap Hywel's character says, in "Gold", "The night was sluttish with stars. My bridal veil / Let in their light in tiny, glittering points", we know that poetry written in the oldest British language still speaks to us; and we may wish to hear more.

Thanks for Listening, People

JOHN REDMOND

Sophie Hannah, *First of the Last Chances*
Carcanet, £4.45, ISBN 1857546261
John Whitworth, *The Whitworth Gun*
Peterloo, £7.95, ISBN 1904324045
Anne Stevenson, *A Report from the Border*
Bloodaxe, £7.95, ISBN 1852246162
Julian Turner, *Crossing the Outskirts*
Anvil, £7.95, ISBN 0856463523
Kevin Hart, *Flame Tree: Selected Poems*
Bloodaxe, £9.95, ISBN 185224545X

TWO CONTRASTING EXAMPLES of Light Verse are offered by Sophie Hannah and John Whitworth. While Hannah is in the domestic mode of Wendy Cope and Pam Ayers, Whitworth offers us a more intellectualized, Auden-flavoured model. Of course it was Auden who made the form more or less respectable again in his 1938 introduction to *The Oxford Book of Light Verse*. Since then, in Auden's helpfully loose definition, approachable poems about everyday life have had a better run for their money. Hannah and Whitworth both rely on the varieties of charm projected by their poetic personae, the former introverted, the latter exuberant. Characteristically, the speaker in a Hannah poem will put herself down. The poems draw on a very recognisable model of English femininity, which keeps its distance while at the same time, in confidential asides, intimating that she is really just one of the gals. This effect is practically the defining quality of the short slight poem, "The Guest Speaker", for example:

I have to keep myself awake
While the guest speaker speaks.
For his and for procedure's sake
I have to keep myself awake.
However long his talk might take
(And, Christ, it feels like weeks)
I have to keep myself awake
While the guest speaker speaks.

The poems maintain the façade of a façade; the self which winks at us, while all the respectable stuff is going on, is just another mask. Like Wendy Cope's work in *If I Don't Know*, the poems state a willingness to be dull, to be lazy, to Just Stay In ("Please can I stay/ Behind? I will if necessary grovel./ I want to stay beside the pool all day") which tends to signal that it's okay for the reader to be lazy too. They hardly ever take up a demanding controversial position. As the Frost-inflected opening poem, "Long for This World" demonstrates, Hannah is capable of writing winningly understated lyric poems, but elsewhere, it seems to me, she too quickly embraces diminished expectations. The poems are highly formulaic – often using an I-persona, in quatrains with *abab* rhyming, the first sentence coincident with the first two lines. Many flesh out relatively slight ideas. "Charge", for example, a pregnancy-poem with military metaphors, builds itself jokily around the phrase having "the stomach for a fight". Similarly "Wells-Next-the-Sea" builds itself around the "missing word" in the name of the Norfolk town: "From time time, every now and then, / I hope meet up with him again."

We pass from Hannah's domesticities to the more phallocentric poems of *The Whitworth Gun*, from poems about pregnancy tests to poems celebrating having sex with boys in showers. Whitworth's poems, which have a much broader range of reference than Hannah's, search far and wide for subject-matter and are not shy about name-dropping (whole poems, for example, are devoted to Auden, Whitman, and John Peel). Auden firmly admitted nonsense poetry to the pantheon of Light Verse and Whitworth has occasional sallies in this direction. "To This My Honeybee", for example, is based around a computer programme's attempt to translate Larkin's "This Be The Verse":

Oh kiss me to the top, my bliss,
Oh kiss me through the tenses!
My jockey cock, once cock-a-hoop,
Gone dainty drupe and soppy-poop,
Still willy-nilly can recoup
Additional expenses,
So fuck up my defences.

Whereas in one poem Hannah proposes that, rather than trying to find a bath in Leeds, it might be better to read Proust, Whitworth, less careful about not seeming to be superior, describes a public bath in terms of an "agreeably Proustian essence". Whitworth is also willing to attack other poets in his poems, and indeed begins *The Whitworth Gun* with just such a broadside, in the sarcastic voice of "Cuddly Wordsmith":

It's now. It's new. It's easy-peasy-poo,
Not that old hard stuff word stuff now-you-see
It-now-you-don't stuff. That stuff's not for you.
Try me. I'm soft. I'm stuffed. I'm poetry.
I'm worth an hour. I'll tell you over lunch.
Thanks for listening, people. Thanks a bunch.

Perhaps necessarily, the poems rely a great deal on broadly-drawn types, and on adapting the resources of popular form – the genre-novel, the cinema, the song. My personal favourite was his well-observed skit on the voices of Test Match Special, which showcases his rhythmical dexterity. Like much of the book, it is a lively, entertaining performance in the best Light Verse tradition.

Anne Stevenson's poetry would not normally be described as Light Verse but her accessible, quick-witted poems of public and private commentary (including one about New York after 9/11) occupy much of the same territory. The appearance of *A Report from the Border* coincides with her seventieth birthday and is evidence of a charitable, vigorous temperament which puts to shame poets half her age. Although the book contains a number of elegies, its tone is rarely dispirited. Her forms are enviably flexible and agreeable, ranging from the neatly squared-off quatrain to stanzas with irregular line-length (almost in the mode of Marianne Moore). While the poems characteristically ironise ambition and seriousness, like Whitworth's, they are cultured, inquiring, and well-read. The subtitle of the book is "New and Rescued Poems" as she revises, in thoroughly Audenesque fashion, some work from her previous volumes. One of these is the touching lyric, "Haunted", which shows her skill with highly compressed statement:

It's not when you walk through my sleep
That I'm haunted most.
I am also alive where you were.
And my own ghost.

Julian Turner's *Crossing the Outskirts* is a more mixed collection. He reaches at times for such stock phrases as "the forest's deep twilight" and "glistening dew" but he is also able to "ng and urr" when sitting in the dentist's chair. An Englishman, who sets a number of affectionate poems in the highlands and islands of Scotland, he tends to become a little saccharine when writing about Nature – to "glory in the rainbow while it fades" as one poem puts it. His style is often stiff. He has, for instance, a fondness for set-pieces, for object-poems like "Whale Bone" and "Tennis Ball" and for landscape poems like "Tenure" and "Walk-On Parts". Usually organized around the five-beat line, he shows a weakness for what Michael Hofmann calls "a freeze-dried descriptiveness" – generalizing, compact lines like "a pre-war world that smells of oil and steam" and "the armorial achievements of the poor". Turner seems at his best and most unbuttoned when writing non-realistic poems based around a daring conceit like "Inside the Panopticon", "Scarecrow Hospital", or "'The Seal People":

they skinned themselves assuming human shape,
their seal-natures pulled up on the sand
like boats beyond the breakers' reach and roar

and built a beacon out of tidewrack where
they cooked the fish they carried in their tails.

Kevin Hart's *Selected Poems* carries on its back cover the mighty endorsement of Harold Bloom praising him as the "most outstanding Australian poet of his generation …". The book, which selects from just over a quarter-century's worth of writing, lives up to this high praise. Despite his academic background (Hart is an English professor in Melbourne) the surface texture of the poems is clear and direct. Underneath, the poems are subtly meditative, carried along by the speaker's attractively restrained voice. He is formally various – experimenting by turns with ghazals, haikus, and prose-poems, but his most noticeable strength is a concentrated descriptiveness such as we find in the opening of "The Real World":

> Rays of sunlight quietly fishing from tall trees;
> A wrestler, smoking, his fingers fat as toes;
> Old men in bars, with arms that end in glass;
> A haloed moon tonight, a hole within a hole.

Hart has an eye for strong opening lines ("The maps of death get better every day –", "Vast cobwebs in the sky. No wind for months", and the wonderful "I forget everything, and make a rat"). Occasionally, the poems remind me too strongly of other poets – Larkin's "At Grass" and "Cut Grass" echo through, respectively, "Flemington Racecourse" and "The Fragrance of Summer Grass" (although these poems are still branded with Hart's distinctive personality). In the poems written after 1990, I thought I could detect the more enabling influence of Charles Wright. Hart and Wright both combine a casual, conversational voice with autobiographical, often long-lined poems, infused by a religious (or in Wright's case at least) a post-religious sensibility. These features are on attractive display in one of Hart's best poems, "Thinking of David Campbell":

> That thick sweet smell of country gums in heat,
> Leaves dangling down,
> And small bright angels hanging high up there,
>
> Asleep, I'd say, most of them, up in the piccolo branches,
> With not a word to say,
> And all of them just lazing there, light passing through their minds,
>
> No sound from heaven,
> No gold mouth opening, but the cicadas still intoning,
> *Light, heat, Monaro noon . . .*

Poet in the Gallery

KARLIEN VAN DEN BEUKEL

Exodus

Photographs by Sebastião Salgado, Barbican Gallery, London

AND THIS, SAID my sister-in-law as she passed round the photographs, is our house.

In the view to the garden, a tree polka-dotted with plums asserted itself cheerfully. The house was nothing but a lot of gaping holes, splinters, ripped electric flex. A forgotten, torn book in the corner of a bedroom (hers, she said). The rest ransacked. Even the window frames had been crowbarred out.

Her family had had to leave their home, which is in a part of Croatia that had been invaded by the Serbs until it was taken back by the Croats, and they had returned to this, the photographs I was now seeing.

What a lovely plum tree, I said. O, the tree, said my sister-in-law. When my parents came back, the neighbours, Serbs who had stayed, came to say they never picked its fruit, wouldn't dream of it. So why did they feel they needed to come say that, she asked.

More and more we will have to find adequate ways to respond to people's experience of forced displacement. In the world, one in 300 of us is now a "person of concern" to the UNHCR. These 19.8 million people represent just those recognised under the mandate of the UNHCR. It is estimated that because of globalisation, social unrest, and economic and political crises, 125 million people are now uprooted from their home country. Many more hundreds of millions are internal migrant workers, moving to the ever-expanding slum areas of megacities in search of basic livelihood. Indeed, the International Labour Organisation points out that, in the wake of economic globalisation, it is increasingly difficult to make the conventional distinction between refugees as defined by the 1951 Convention and people displaced because of other compelling circumstances. Increasing numbers of uprooted people fall outside the protective reach of international humanitarian law.

Chattelised women walking across a mountainous terrain in Ecuador; people clinging to the sides of train carriages in India; a child's face behind the shattered glass of a coach in Krajina; Rwandan refugees walking in line on one side of a dusty road, the other side lined with the dead; North African young men pressed together in a dinghy blinking into the coastguard's searchlight.

Sebastião Salgado's exhibition *Exodus* allows us, if not to come to terms with, then at least to begin to recognise the critical global scale of these unprecedented mass migrations. The photographer, renowned for his reportage of migrant workers in the Brazilian gold-mines, travelled to over 40 countries between 1993 and 1999, registering human migrations as they occurred. The exhibition is organised into five sections, including people's flight from environmental distress in Honduras and Ecuador; from violence and war in former Yugoslavia, Rwanda, Angola, and Afghanistan; moving from depleted subsistence plots to the new megacities in India, Brazil, and Mexico. As a campaigning photographer, Salgado would like his vast documentary project to initiate a wider public discussion on the shared experience of all displaced people:

I shoot globally and I want to show globally: each of my stories is about globalization and economic liberalization: a sample of the human condition on the planet today. My big hope is to aid and provoke a debate so that we can discuss the human condition looking from the point of view of displaced peoples around the world. My photographs are like a vector that link what is happening and give the person who does not have the opportunity to go there the possibility to look.

There are many ways of looking at these photographs; and there are so many photographs that you can't look at them all. In intellectual terms, I am not convinced that the central tenet of the exhibition – that each of the stories of displaced people is linked – is all that helpful when, in real terms, different local complexities need to be painstakingly examined and negotiated in order to come to practical solutions and resolutions. The exhibition's central tenet is given particular emotional force in the final section: rows of portraits of luminously-eyed, serious children, identified just by the date and location of their refugee camp, detention centre, or orphanage. The cumulative effect is tight-throat overwhelming: it is easy to know how to respond within the terms of its direct appeal.

With my-sister-in-law it is complicated, because neither of us know the terms. She has to find a way to talk to me, and me to her, through everything else, and then we kind of do. In fact, I was reminded of my "O what a lovely plum tree" remark, because Salgado's black-and-white photographs are very beautiful even as, at times, they convey human distress.

"Society clothes the places of misery with Romanticism in order to render them eternal", Siegfried Kracauer once remarked. Some would argue that the aesthetic distances us from the suffering and hardship it seeks to portray. Yet this presumes that aesthetic sensibility is the prerogative of the privileged. Whilst Salgado is a master of the tenebrist grandeur of landscape, many compositions reveal the aesthetic innate in the handiwork of the people he photographed. They may have few possessions but the clothes on their back, but in Salgado's work these become visual signifiers of personal dignity and culture under the bleakest of conditions. His mediation of people's everyday ceremoniousness, the way they are able to create order in make-shift surroundings, encourages a constructive social vision.

In the Rwandan refugee camp, Benako, Tanzania, 1994, a man is stitching a piece of white cloth on his Singer, out in the open, among the makeshift tents, bundles, and shacks. His clothes are elegant, a jacket in a Prince of Wales check and a matching checked cap, chosen with a sartorial eye for expert pattern-cutting. What he is stitching the white cloth into is unknown – a flag, a bandage, a shroud – indeed, the fate of this man is unknown to us.

Yet his care allows us to consider the photographer's craft more closely too. Salgado's visual narrative seems reminiscent of Caravaggio, not just in its use of light, but also in its biblical composition of displaced people.

In the Rwandan refugee camp at Benato, Tanzania, children play on a mound of earth dug up to make latrines. They pose themselves into a cherubic mountain, two small children still clambering up, holding each other for support.

At the Katale camp, Goma, Zaire, a young man with a bare torso and unseeing wide eyes, is cradled in a woman's lap. It looks like a Pietà. In his left extended arm, a small drip.

A young girl in a headscarf has gathered wood, pale branches gathered in the shape of a cross.

Hutu refugees are fleeing into the jungle. You see the backs of the heads of the people in front of you, carefully finding their way through the dense undergrowth. They are carrying a dead man on a stretcher. You could almost be one of those bearers, the composition draws you in so close.

Like church paintings, Salgado's photographs have a didactic purpose, but a modern one: to illuminate humanitarian values. In the end, they may ask only something very simple of us: to give – and to think about the real complexities later.

The Barbican art gallery has invited poets to present their work and discuss their responses to the Salgado exhibition on May 7, 14, 21, and 28 at 7pm. Participating poets include John Agard, Natan Barreto, Debjani Chatterjee, Kaiser Haq, Andrew Motion, Beverley Naidoo, Grace Nichols, Olusola Oyeleye, Michael Rosen, Mimi Khalvati, Jo Shapcott, George Szirtes, and Timberlake Wertenbaker.

Please telephone 0845 120 7550 for more information and tickets. The exhibition runs until 1 June 2003.

SEBASTIAO SALGADO / AMAZONAS IMAGES / *NB PICTURES

National Poetry Competition

The first, second and third prize-winners in the National Poetry Competition 2002 are listed below. Prizes totalled £6,500 in cash, plus publication of the winning poems in *Poetry Review*. The judges were Simon Armitage, Suzi Feay (Chair), Selima Hill, and Hugo Williams.

First Prize   *Julia Copus*

BREAKING THE RULE

I. The Art of Illumination

At times it is a good life, with the evening sun
gilding the abbey tower, the brook's cold waters

sliding past and every hour in my Book
a blank page, vellum pumice-stoned

to chalky lustres which my inks suffuse:
saffron and sandarach and dragon's blood,

azure and verdigris. Monsters and every type of beast
curl round the words. Each man here has a past,

and each man reasons for his faith. I wronged
a woman once and nothing I did after could atone

or throw a light upon the blackness of that deed,
whose harm lay in the telling, not the doing.

My floor is strewn with thyme and rosemary
to mask the odours of my craft – fish glue,

gum resins, vinegar and oils. With these I shape
the host of the redeemed, and every face

takes on the features of a face I've known
and every angel's face beneath the shadow

of its many coloured wings is hers alone.

II The Art of Signing

There are ways among the stone and shadow
of our cloisters to transgress the Rule We speak

in signs: a language with no syntax.
For the sign of bread you make a circle

with your thumbs and index fingers – like a belt
that presses silk against a woman's waist.

For the sign of an eel squeeze each hand tight
as one who grasps a cord of hair to kiss

that one mouth only in the frantic din
of the ale-house where we used to dance,

and later outside with the grainy dusk
unloading a sough of foot-falls in my ear,

our four feet shuffling together
and in time across the quiet earth.

The rhythm of my days goes slower now:
matins and lauds, vespers and compline.

For the sign of silence put a finger
to the dry muscle of your mouth,

the darkness that's inside it. Keep it there.

Second Prize   *David Hart*

THEN IN THE TWENTIETH CENTURY

Then in the twentieth century they invented transparent adhesive tape,
the first record played on Radio 1 was *Flowers In The Rain* by the Move,
and whereas ink had previously been in pots, now it was in cartridges.

They killed each other a lot and found ingenious and crafty ways to do it,
sometimes one person got killed, sometimes eleven, sometimes ninety-eight,
and some of the new equipment managed a million or more, it was, friends,

spectacular. Seymour, Foggy and Blamire gave audiences week by week
a chuckle, between 1941 and 1958 the New York Yankees won the world series
ten times, I did my A Levels, failed Physics twice, got Chemistry and Zoology,

and cycled a lot and drew maps. C. Day Lewis wrote a poem, *The Tourists*,
and George Steiner said, 'We must all learn to be guests of each other',
I decided, in making my own poems, against punch lines, and lost in stages all

of my upper teeth. Peter Sutcliffe in 1987 confessed to thirteen murders,
when I was young we had no television, but we did have ice cream in cones.
Redundant churches became clubs, community centres, galleries or homes,

the phrase 'The best thing since sliced bread' (or not) got into the language,
Sir Basil Spence won the competition to build the new Coventry Cathedral,
I was born by the sea then lived in cities, Matisse in his old age made cut-outs.

One afternoon at precisely four-twenty, on the corner of Corporation Street,
wearing old jeans and a new red jacket, sheltering in a shop front from the rain,
she saw a man stab another man to death, blood everywhere, people screaming.

Men quarrelled about scrolls found in pots near the Dead Sea, the library
at Norwich burned down, milk was pasteurised by law, I have four children,
all adult now, small islands became uninhabited, Harpo never spoke on film.

Matthew Caley

LOW MAINTENANCE ROOF GARDEN

We take the air out of our low-maintenance roof garden
this austere quad our best line of defence
from the smoky street where we hear arteries harden.

Honesty seems a new form of pretence
for here is hardly either Avalon or Eden.
Yet this gravel reach can seem a wild expanse.

We splay on deckchairs wilting in the sun,
as window-boxes bear the flowering quince,
the flowering plum. We live above neon, shop signs, gargoyles, gorgons.

If you leap or joy do not leap over the fence
of our low maintenance roof-garden
as one did once and some have done so since.

The street below. The sky above. The garden inbetween
with only barren stones as any sustenance,
mica-chips, wave-smoothed glass, obsidian –

we lie on these hard stones doing penance
for not having a warm shoulder to cry on.
A shingle beach half way up the sky has the appearance

of the temporary. Yet we mark our territory aeon after aeon
and reacquaint ourselves with innocence,
lying between the stars and Municipal bins.

If there's anything to take we take it on sufferance.
Taking the air of our roof-garden.
It's night. We hear a noise. Pardon? What? The noise is silence

or dawn bringing the black hat of the traffic warden
to pin the law on the windscreen's crazy fluorescence
below. We sit tight in our low-maintenance roof-garden.

Editorial Notelet

It hasn't been our habit, since taking over the editorship of *Poetry Review*, to write editorials. Our idea has been that, for the time being at any rate, the magazine's poems, essays, and reviews are best left speaking for themselves. Perhaps as a consequence of this – the absence of a quarterly position statement – the *Poetry Review* letters page has ceased to exist.

Not that we haven't had letters. We've had plenty of letters; many of our correspondents, the great majority in fact, writing with enthusiasm about the new direction (or directions) the magazine is taking. Some people, naturally, have been critical of changes we have made, and we would like to thank these correspondents for their thoughtfulness and courtesy. As yet, however, we haven't had a single letter marked "For Publication". This seems a shame.

We would like, therefore, to invite the revival of the *Poetry Review* letters page. We are confident we can rely on readers to make the most of this opportunity.

The Poetry Library is 50 years old this year. *Poetry Review* congratulates the library on its invaluable and continuing contribution to the nation's culture.

The Poetry Library

The Poetry Library is the most comprehensive collection of modern poetry in Britain containing all twentieth and twenty-first century work published in the UK, a huge selection from other English speaking countries and an unrivalled collection of translations. Come and explore poetry books, poetry on cassette, CD, video and CD-ROM, poetry magazines and much more!

"Use and enjoy this place. Burrow in. Borrow on"
– John Hegley

Membership of the Poetry Library is free.
Telephone 0207 9210943/0664
Email poetrylibrary@rfh.org.uk
The Poetry Library, Level 5,
Royal Festival Hall, London SE1